Balancing Act

For People with Dizziness and Balance Disorders

Second Edition

By Mary Ann V
Helen Sinclair,
and P. J. Haybach

Printed in the United States of America.

Published by the Vestibular Disorders Association
PO Box 13305
Portland, OR 97213-0305
(800) 837-8428
info@vestibular.org
www.vestibular.org

Second Edition
Printed in the United States of America
10 9 8 7 6 5 4 3 2

ISBN 10: 0-9632611-5-0
ISBN 13: 978-0-9632611-5-1

Table of Contents

Preface

People who are affected by disorders that are not well understood by the public or by many health care professionals must become their own advocates. Accordingly, we wrote this book to provide you with information so that you can begin to understand your dizziness and related symptoms, to get help for them, to learn to compensate for them, and to educate others about it.

We use quotations and situations to illustrate our discussion. These are not direct quotes or actual situations but are based on information shared with us by hundreds of patients, families, and health professionals. The names we use are fictional.

This book is not intended to provide medical advice. Qualified professionals should be consulted whenever specific advice is needed.

Not all professionals are knowledgeable about or able to diagnose and treat all kinds of dizziness. We refer to health professionals who have been trained specifically to help you, but we recognize that it may be difficult to find people with this expertise. We hope you will use *Balancing Act* as a general guide to asking the right questions, finding the answers, and getting the help you need.

Acknowledgments

This book would not have been possible without the assistance of a great many people and organizations, including the medical and scientific advisors and the board of directors of the Vestibular Disorders Association. We are grateful to all who contributed to the completion of this project.

Joyce Sherman, co-owner of River Graphics, Portland, Oregon, designed the book and prepared the index.

Chapter 1

Introduction

Dizziness is not a disease. It is a symptom—a warning that you have a problem.

Dizziness means different things to different people. One person might use the word "dizziness" to mean lightheadedness, while to another person it means something like the spinning of a merry-go-round. Others might say it feels as though the Earth is spinning under their feet or that their feet don't move the way they should. People sometimes use it interchangeably with the term "vertigo," though vertigo is only one kind of dizziness. They may use it to describe mild turning, imbalance, or feelings of faintness. In ordinary use, the term "dizziness" is therefore somewhat vague, though we would probably all say we know what it's like to be dizzy.

Your dizziness may be quite mild or very severe. It may be severe enough to diminish your quality of life, to keep you from holding a job, or to prevent you from maintaining your household. It can be economically and socially devastating if it stems from a cause that is difficult to treat.

Severe chronic or episodic dizziness affects all aspects of your life. We all understand that dizziness causes imbalance and unsteadiness. Do you realize that dizziness often results in an inability to concentrate and a loss of short-term memory?

You may find it difficult to read, especially long articles or a book. Sometimes you won't be able to recall words you want to use in a conversation. You may even forget simple directions or instructions. These difficulties result from increased high-level brain activity. Your brain is "working overtime" to overcome the effects of a malfunctioning balance system that normally works automatically.

Your own experiences with dizziness have probably taught you that you always need to make flexible plans. Perhaps canceling your Friday night bowling, your box seats for the ballet, or your dinner with friends has made you feel as if you're losing your social life. No matter what you want to do, you know you have to be able to get out of it at the last minute if you're feeling dizzy. Coping with dizziness or the threat of dizziness has to be your first priority.

You may have had some unpleasant experiences in public. Have you ever become disoriented in a shopping mall when the busy crowds of people, the noise, and the lights have been too confusing? Maybe you've fallen once or twice. You rationalized it as clumsiness at first, but now that it's happened again the unpleasant memory of your embarrassment and your insecurity keep you from venturing out alone.

Perhaps you are afraid to leave home by yourself. Do you often have to depend on others to drive, to shop, and to do things for you that you've always done for yourself?

You may feel your independence slipping away. Family and friends don't always understand.

Do any of the following sound familiar?

- "I don't see why Judy never wants to play tennis with the group any more."
- "He looks perfectly healthy to me."
- "Personally, I think her 'dizziness' is all in her head."
- "He just says that to get attention."
- "Frankly, I'm getting tired of the same old excuse."

Your doctors may not have a solution to your problem either. How many times have you been told, "You need to learn to relax"? Stress, depression, and everything from eyestrain to brain tumors are among the potential causes that may have been suggested for your dizziness. And even if your physician has finally pinpointed the specific cause, there may be no indication that he or she understands how your symptoms affect you emotionally. Sometimes you feel angry and completely frustrated because no one knows what you're going through.

You have to cope with your physical problems, with mental fatigue, and with lack of understanding from your family, your friends, and the medical profession. This adds enormous stress to your life. Combined with this stress is uncertainty about your health and future.

Will I ever get well? Why can't I do things I want to do? What's wrong with me? Why do I feel so dizzy?

You need to find out what is causing your dizziness and what you can do to control it.

The early chapters of this book raise many questions and start you in the right direction to find answers. You will learn some basic facts about your balance system, the more common causes of dizziness, the most common balance disorders, and up-to-date treatment methods.

The later chapters offer many suggestions for controlling your dizziness, particularly if treatment isn't helping enough, from managing attacks to organizing your work place. Here you will find the kind of information you need to help you to help yourself. Finally, we've included information about where you can learn more about balance disorders and how you can help educate your family, friends, and acquaintances about these life-altering conditions.

Chapter 2

Dizziness and the Balance System

W hen you are healthy, you can keep your balance because a coordinating center for balance in your brainstem continually evaluates the input it receives from at least three sensory systems—your eyes, your muscles and joints, and your vestibular system. The brainstem receives this input in the form of innumerable sensory nerve impulses.

In response to the input, your brainstem sends motor nerve impulses to your eye muscles to allow clear vision as you move and to your body muscles to allow you to sit, to stand, to walk, even to turn cartwheels and still maintain your balance.

Sensory Input to the Brainstem

Sensory receptors in your eyes are sensitive to changes in the light waves that strike them. When the receptors are stimulated by light, they initiate impulses in the nerve fibers attached to them. The nerve impulses travel through fibers of the optic nerves from your eyes to the balance center in your brainstem. Sensory impulses from your eyes provide your brainstem with continuous information about your surroundings—buildings aligned straight up and down, or cars zipping by in traffic.

Sensory receptors in your muscles and joints called *proprioceptors* are sensitive to changes in the tissues surrounding them. When touch, pressure, or movement stimulate the receptors, they initiate sensory impulses in the nerve fibers attached to them. These impulses travel through nerves to your spinal cord and brain and provide your brainstem with continuous information about the surfaces you are touching or standing on—a brick wall, a gravel walkway, or a boat deck.

Your vestibular system provides the most important input to your brainstem: information about changes in your head position with respect to gravity.

The objects you see around you and the surfaces you touch or stand on may be changing continually. The sensory input your brainstem receives from your senses of vision and proprioception may be in conflict with one another. (For example, when you are standing next to a moving bus and you feel as though you are moving, too.) In these instances the brainstem places highest priority on the input it receives from your vestibular system. Your vestibular system is providing information about the only unchanging point of reference available to your balance system: the force of gravity, or Earth vertical.

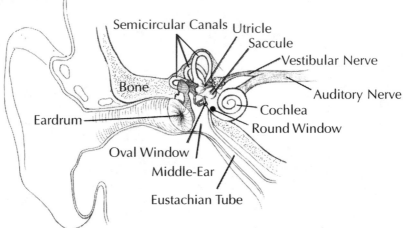

Figure 2-1: The ear

The inner ear (or labyrinth) is a complex system of chambers and passageways in the bone of the skull. Within the bony labyrinth lie interconnected thin-walled sacs and tubes filled with a fluid called endolymph and surrounded by a different fluid, perilymph.

The hearing portion of the labyrinth is the cochlea. The balance portion is the vestibular system.

The vestibular system in each inner ear consists of three semicircular canals and two chambers, the utricle and saccule.

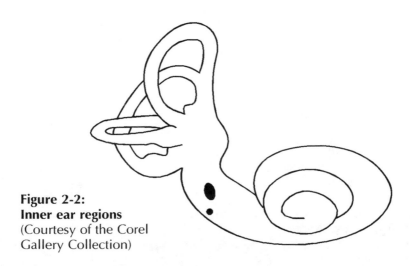

Figure 2-2:
Inner ear regions
(Courtesy of the Corel
Gallery Collection)

The three semicircular canals lie at right angles to each other and to those on the opposite side of the head. This permits detection of changes in angular or rotational movement of the head in all directions. The movement may be either active (turning your head, doing a cartwheel) or passive (whirling around on a carnival ride).

Each semicircular canal is partitioned by a cupula containing sensory receptors called hair cells. A hair cell is a specialized cell that has cilia (hair-like projections) protruding from one end. When your head is rotating (either speeding up or slowing down) in the direction of a certain canal, the fluid within that canal lags behind and presses against the cupula, thereby bending its hair cells. When your head is stationary or when it is moving at a constant speed, the cupula (with hair cells) remains stationary because the fluid "catches up" and moves at the same speed as your head.

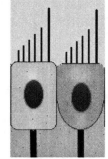

Figure 2-3:
Hair cells

As the hair cells bend, they initiate impulses in the nerve endings attached to them. These sensory nerve impulses travel over the vestibular nerves to the brainstem.

Within both the utricle and saccule is a macula, a patch of hair cells coated with a gelatinous layer that contains small granules called otoliths or otoconia. The macular organs, also known as otolithic organs, respond to head movement in a certain plane. The macula in the utricle responds to head motion in the direction of Earth horizontal and the macula in the saccule to Earth vertical.

As head position changes either actively (tipping your head) or passively (moving upward in an elevator), the otoliths in the saccule are pulled in the direction of Earth by gravity. The gelatinous layer moves with them and in turn bends the hair cells. As horizontal head

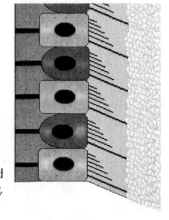

Figure 2-4:
Group of hair cells while head is upright and still. Also, group of hair cells, cilia bent by gravity, as head moves to side-lying position.

motion changes (walking, sitting motionless in a moving car), the otoliths in the utricle, because they are heavier than the fluid surrounding them, lag behind, pulling the gelatinous layer with them and bending the hair cells. (Figure 2-5 gives an overview of the sensory receptors of the vestibular system.)

When the hair cells are bent, they stimulate the sensory nerve endings at their bases. As a result of stimulation, nerve impulses are sent along the vestibular nerves that connect the maculae to the brainstem.

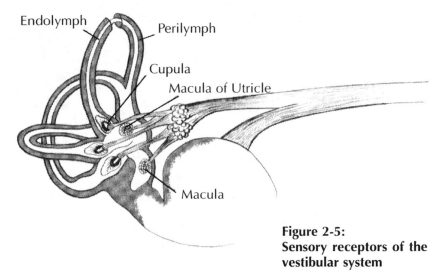

Figure 2-5:
Sensory receptors of the
vestibular system

The direction and type of head movement determine exactly which nerve endings are stimulated. Under normal conditions, the impulses going to the brain from the right and left side of the vestibular system are symmetrical (that is, the input from the right side conforms with input from the left side.)

Your brainstem also receives input from higher levels of your brain, those involved with memory and thinking. This input influences the brainstem's activity as all of the sensory impulses to the balance center are sorted out.

Motor Output from the Brainstem

In the brainstem, the sensory nerve impulses from your vestibular system, your eyes, and your proprioceptors are relayed to motor nerve fibers that originate in your brainstem. These fibers carry motor nerve impulses from the brainstem to all the muscles of your body.

Vestibulo-Ocular Reflex (VOR)

Some motor nerve impulses from the balance center go to the muscles attached to your eyeballs. These nerve impulses coordinate eye movements with head movements so that you can have clear vision while your head is moving either actively or passively. The normal pattern of coordinated eye movement that occurs with extreme head movements is called nystagmus. Under normal conditions, when head movements are small or slow, nystagmus does not occur.

Vestibulo-Spinal Reflex (VSR)

Other motor nerve impulses are sent from the brainstem through the spinal cord to the muscles of your head and neck, your arms and legs, and the rest of your body. These nerve impulses control the movement of your skeletal muscles and coordinate their actions so you can keep your balance, whether you are sitting, standing, turning cartwheels, or riding your bicycle.

"Normal" Dizziness

Under normal circumstances, balance control takes place at an unconscious level. Once you learn to stand, to walk, and to turn cartwheels, you don't think about all the muscle actions necessary to carry out these activities.

When there is any departure from the normal sensory input that your brainstem is used to receiving, impulses are immediately referred to the cerebral cortex, the conscious level of your brain. As a result, you become aware of the abnormal input. This usually produces a sensation of dizziness.

People who are not prone to motion sickness normally can adapt to unusual input after a time. For example, if you are a landlubber going to sea, you may feel dizzy and seasick at first. Your brainstem is not accustomed to receiving the amounts and kinds of input it is receiving because of the rolling and pitching of your boat. But after a few days your balance center adapts to the unusual input, the seasick feelings go away, and you "get your sea legs." You may also experience dizziness when you step off the boat and readapt to normal conditions. Prolonged sensations of movement after a long sea voyage are known as mal de debarquement syndrome.

Normal dizziness results from departures from the usual sensory input caused by changes in your environment. When there doesn't seem to be an environmental cause for your dizziness, something else must be interfering with the normal function of your balance system.

Chapter 3

Causes of Dizziness

D izziness is not unusual. After lower back pain, dizziness is the second most common complaint heard in doctors' offices. At some time in their lives, a large percentage of the adult population reports episodes of dizziness or rotary feelings of vertigo to physicians. Many of these cases involve inner ear disorders, while others involve disorders unrelated to the inner ear. In some cases, the underlying cause remains unknown or involves a combination of factors.

Vestibular Disorders

In many of the people suffering from dizziness or vertigo, the cause is a disturbance in the vestibular apparatus of one or both inner ears. These parts of your anatomy provide your brain with information about changes in head movement with respect to the pull of gravity and help you to maintain balance and an upright posture.

When your vestibular system is not functioning properly, the result may be dizziness, vertigo, imbalance, spatial disorientation, and perhaps nausea and vomiting.

Unknown Causes

In many cases of vestibular disorders, the underlying or original cause cannot be determined. This is true of Meniere's disease, of many cases of BPPV, and some cases of bilateral loss, and may be true in other cases.

Infection

Infection can cause vestibular problems. Viral infections of the labyrinth (labyrinthitis) or the vestibular nerve (vestibular neuronitis) are fairly common. Labyrinthitis can include hearing and vestibular problems, while vestibular neuronitis affects only vestibular function.

Bacterial infection of either the middle ear (otitis media) or the brain coverings (meningitis) can spread to the inner ear and cause widespread permanent damage, including deafness and balance impairments.

A non-infecting inflammation of the inner ear, serious labyrinthitis, can also occur on occasion in conjunction with a middle ear infection and after ear surgery.

Allergies

Generally speaking, people who have inner ear disorders or ear damage and allergies can experience increased symptoms during the allergy season. Allergic reactions may cause some kinds of vestibular dysfunction in the first place or can make an existing vestibular problem feel worse. These reactions may cause changes in the inner ear fluids and may also change middle ear pressures because of swelling of the eustachian tube and production of fluid in the middle ear.

Head Trauma

In people under age 50, a common cause of inner ear damage that results in dizziness, vertigo, and/or hearing loss is head injury. This might involve an actual blow to the head or a "whiplash" injury. One or both inner ears may be involved.

The severity and duration of symptoms depend on the location and extent of damage to the vestibular system. Although the victim's symptoms may begin immediately following head trauma, sometimes they are not apparent at the time of injury. Days, weeks, or months later, the person may experience gradual or sudden hearing loss, dizziness, and vertigo.

Ototoxins

An ototoxin is any substance that can poison the ear. (Oto = ear. Toxin = poison.) This poisoning sometimes happens when people come into contact with certain drugs or chemicals. The poisoning does not involve the outer or middle ears; it affects the inner ear and/or the vestibulo-cochlear nerve. Because the inner ear is responsible for both hearing and balance information, ototoxins can disturb or damage either or both of these senses.

Aging

There is evidence to suggest that in some cases the structures of the inner ear, including the vestibular hair cells, degenerate as a person grows older. Dizziness, vertigo, and hearing loss may occur. People older than 65 have an increased chance of developing BPPV.

Tumor of the Vestibulo-Cochlear Nerve

Occasionally, a slow-growing tumor on the vestibulo-cochlear nerve from the inner ear to the brain may interfere with the normal function of the balance system. Abnormal messages from the vestibular system to the brain cause sensations of dizziness or vertigo.

Motion Sickness

Motion sickness may affect anyone with intact vestibular system function. Only people without vestibular function are completely immune to motion sickness. However, if your vestibular system is damaged or the function of your vestibular system is altered without complete loss of vestibular function, you will be more prone to motion sickness.

Motion sickness occurs when you are exposed to unusual or conflicting orientation references. When this happens, unusual or conflicting sensory input from your eyes, proprioceptors, and/or vestibular system is sent to your brainstem. When the input is referred to the cerebral cortex, you become aware of it, and you feel dizzy or motion-sick.

For instance, when you are driving on a windy, rough road, your vestibular system is continually sending input concerning the twists and turns, bounces and jolts, to your brainstem. When this unusual sensory input is referred to the conscious level of your brain, you feel motion-sick.

Sometimes you may be able to overcome motion sickness. When you sit in a moving vehicle, focus on a distant point straight ahead or on an object inside the vehicle, whichever makes you feel most comfortable and creates the least symptoms (nausea). By minimizing disturbing visual input (for example, motion in your peripheral field of vision) you may be able to reduce or avoid the effects of motion sickness.

People who are prone to motion sickness can sometimes prevent the symptoms by using anti-motion sickness medications (vestibular suppressants) such as Bonine, Dramamine Original, Dramamine Less Drowsy, Antivert, and Marezine, which are over-the-counter medications available in most drug stores. Your physician may also prescribe the use of transdermal scopolamine patches, which are placed on the skin behind the ear. The medications should be taken before you begin your trip. Check with your doctor to find out how far in advance you should take them.

Other Causes

In some of the people who complain to their physicians of dizziness, the cause may be visual disturbances, eye movement disorders, lack of blood flow to the brainstem, or severe dehydration. Diseases of the heart or blood vessels or disorders of the nervous system may also cause dizziness.

Visual Disturbances

Lightheadedness or dizziness affects some people when their visual reference points aren't accurate. They may get dizzy when they look straight up to see clouds moving in the sky or when they are standing on high bridges. People who are afraid of heights may even feel as though they are falling when they are in high places. Anxiety is often associated with this kind of spatial disorientation, but it is rarely, if ever, the primary cause of dizziness.

If you are affected by these sensations, you may be able to overcome them. Focus on something close by that you know provides an accurate reference to earth vertical (a bridge pier, a window frame). Your brain will receive more visual information, and the dizzy sensation should pass.

Anything that interferes with normal vision has the potential to cause dizziness. It is not uncommon for people to feel dizzy for a while when they are adjusting to bifocals or some other new eyeglass prescription. Cataracts may also reduce vision enough so that dizziness or imbalance results.

Stress and Fatigue

Dizziness may also occur as a result of stress, tension, or fatigue. Under these conditions, the brainstem functions less efficiently, and there is some loss of automatic reflex control of balance. The activity of the conscious level of your brain, the cerebral cortex, must increase to help maintain balance by controlling voluntary muscle movements. As a result of excess higher-level brain activity, you begin to feel lightheaded, unsteady on your feet, or dizzy.

Hyperventilation

Hyperventilation can also cause temporary dizziness.

Brain cells are very sensitive to the concentrations of oxygen and carbon dioxide in the blood.

When you hyperventilate, you breathe rapidly, allowing your body to expel more carbon dioxide than normal during respiration. A lower than normal concentration of carbon dioxide in your blood alters the function of your brain cells. As a result, you feel dizzy.

Slowing your breathing rate or exhaling and inhaling into a paper bag usually corrects this condition quickly.

Decreased Blood Flow to the Brain

Decreased blood flow to the brain, especially the brainstem, may also cause dizziness. Efficient blood circulation to the brain is essential to maintain normal brain cell function.

If blood flow to the brain decreases and insufficient oxygen reaches the cells, the brain cells stop functioning properly. They send inaccurate messages to your brainstem and you feel dizzy.

Orthostatic hypotension

One cause of decreased blood flow to the brain may be orthostatic hypotension (low blood pressure), which may cause fainting or a feeling of faintness when you suddenly rise from a lying or sitting position. If you experience this kind of dizziness it is important to take your time getting out of bed and to avoid standing up suddenly.

Dehydration

Another cause of decreased blood flow to the brain is severe dehydration. It may result from excess loss of fluids because of exercise, hot weather, or fever. Some people may need to drink more fluids, especially water or fruit juice, or they may need a balanced salt solution such as Gatorade or Pedialyte.

Vasovagal syndrome

Vasovagal syndrome is a nervous system response that causes sudden loss of muscle tone in peripheral blood vessels. A vasovagal attack results in pooling of blood in the legs and trunk and may also be a cause of low blood flow to the brain. Sitting down and placing your head between your knees will usually restore blood flow to the brain and relieve the dizzy feeling.

Arteriosclerosis

Arteriosclerosis, the hardening or narrowing of blood vessels, may cause decreased blood flow to the brain that results in dizziness.

Osteoarthritis

Osteoarthritis, or joint disease, in the neck or cervical area of the spine, may also cause dizziness. Openings in the neck vertebrae contain arteries that supply the brain with blood. Osteoarthritis may narrow these openings and restrict blood flow to the brain. This restricted flow can cause dizziness.

Other Nervous System Disorders

Diminished nerve function in the legs or feet (peripheral neuropathies) may cause unsteadiness and difficulty with standing or walking. In rare cases, a tumor may affect the brainstem, the coordination center of the brain (cerebellum) or part of the cerebral cortex that controls voluntary muscle movements. Any of these problems may cause imbalance or dizziness.

If your symptoms are related to one of these nervous system

disorders, a complete medical history and careful neurologic testing can reveal the exact cause.

Chapter 4

Seeking Help

S ome kinds of dizziness are temporary and can be traced easily to identifiable causes. Although these episodes are frightening, there are times when dizziness is a normal occurrence caused by a change in environment, not a physical disorder. In all cases of dizziness, every potential cause should be fully investigated.

If you experience sudden, severe dizziness, and if your symptoms persist or incapacitate you, you should seek medical advice. The place to start is with your family physician or internist. You may need a complete physical examination to determine if your dizziness is related to a circulatory problem, a nervous system disorder, or a disease such as multiple sclerosis.

If your physician determines that the cause of your dizziness is most likely a disorder of your inner ear, you may be referred to a specialist. Physicians who specialize in all of the disorders and diseases of the ear, nose, throat, sinuses, head, and neck are called otolaryngologists. Those MDs specializing solely in disorders and diseases of the ear are otologists, and physicians specializing solely in disorders and diseases of the inner ear are neurotologists or sometimes may be called otoneurologists.

Describing Your Dizziness

So that your physician can gain a clear understanding of your dizziness problem, you must be able to explain your symptoms and the history of your dizziness clearly and in an orderly sequence. A detailed medical history is one of the most important diagnostic tools your doctor uses in determining what is causing your dizziness.

It is difficult to describe what "being dizzy" means. But you can help your doctor if you can describe the events that occur when you feel dizzy. Below are several categories of questions to ask yourself.

Prior Events
- What were the circumstances prior to your first dizziness episode?
- Have you been ill just prior to your first episode, even with only a cold or flu?
- Have you fallen or received a head blow recently?
- Have you recently received intravenous antibiotics?
- Have you ever been unconscious as a result of a head injury?

- Does your family recall that you had problems with dizziness or that you were uncoordinated as a child?

First Attack

- When did your first attack of dizziness occur?
- Describe it in detail.
- Did you fall to the floor or just feel light-headed and unstable?
- If the first episode that you can recall was quite severe, do you remember times before that when you felt slightly dizzy or disoriented?

Duration of Episodes

- Does your dizziness occur in episodes or is it constant?
- How often do the attacks occur?
- How long do they last, by estimate or by measurement with a clock?
- Between acute attacks do you experience any symptoms, or do you usually feel well?

Symptoms

- Would you describe your dizziness as unsteadiness, as light-headedness, or as a rotary feeling (vertigo)?
- If you experience vertigo, during an acute attack does everything revolve around you? Or are you spinning while your surroundings are motionless?
- Do you feel as though you are being pulled toward one side?
- If you have been experiencing periods of dizziness for some time, have the attacks gradually been getting worse?
- Are there any other symptoms that you associate with your dizziness episodes?
- Do you feel pressure or fullness in your head or ears?
- Do you hear ringing or other noises at the time of your attacks?
- Do you notice any decrease in your hearing either during the attacks or following them?
- Do you become nauseated and vomit?

Related Situations

- Can you identify anything that seems to bring on your attacks, such as bending over, turning your head in a specific direction, or lying in bed on one side or the other?
- Does eating a certain food seem to cause dizziness episodes?
- Are you prone to motion sickness? Do swings, merry-go-rounds, and carnival rides make you feel nauseous?

The more specifically you describe your dizziness and other symptoms, the more helpful you will be as your physician attempts to uncover the cause for your problem. Don't be overly concerned about your inability to describe your symptoms if they seem vague or if they seem to change. Simply do the best you can.

If you have been affected by dizziness for some time and you have been diagnosed by physicians in the past, carefully review all your past evaluations, recommended treatments, and the results of those treatments. Your current physician must have access to all your prior medical histories, test results, diagnostic evaluations, and recommendations. Your doctor will ask you to sign authorization forms for obtaining medical records from your previous physicians, clinics, or hospitals. This will make sure that your past medical information becomes part of your current medical file. In addition, you should try to relate any details about how closely you followed your previous physician's directions, how effective each suggestion was, and how your condition changed after each treatment.

Chapter 5

Examination and Testing

A lthough a complete medical history is an important part of diagnosis, many questions about your problem cannot be answered without the results of certain diagnostic tests. The information that your doctor obtains from an examination and your medical history about your symptoms and the circumstances surrounding your dizziness episodes may indicate that specific tests are necessary to obtain data he or she needs to diagnose your problem and to help you.

Most physicians who specialize in diseases and disorders of the ear will test you using several traditional testing procedures.

Although you may have been subjected to extensive testing in the past, better testing procedures are being developed all the time. Especially if some time has passed since you have been tested, your physician may want to repeat some previous tests as well as try newer diagnostic procedures.

External Ear Exam

The external ear canal can be examined directly for obstruction by things such as wax, infection, or foreign bodies. The tympanic membrane (ear drum) can be checked for holes (perforations), signs of fluid or infection in the middle ear, and for a middle ear growth called a cholesteatoma.

Brain and Nervous System Exam

Your doctor will check the function and condition of your brain indirectly by checking a number of things such as how well you can answer questions, how your eyes move, what your eye pupils look like and how they react to light, and how you move muscles around your face. The doctor may also check your muscle strength and coordination and your reflexes and might also test your senses of smell, taste, touch, and vision.

Balance and Movement Exam

For a quick look at your balance function, your doctor will have you stand with your feet side by side and eyes closed or with one foot in front of the other and might also have you "march in place," stand on one foot, or stand on your toes. The doctor may also push you a bit while you are standing. He or she will have you walk in your normal way, may ask you to walk by placing one foot in front of the other or heel to toe, and may have you walk backwards. Possibly, you may be asked to stand on a cushion or walk on something soft.

Eye Movement Exam

Your doctor will observe your eyes for nystagmus while your head is still, when you are moving your head, when you are following his finger with your eyes, and possibly when he or she is moving your head or when you are in different positions. The examiner may check your vision with a standard wall chart while you stand still or possibly while you move your head. You might be asked to put on a pair of glasses or goggles. These magnify your eyes for the examiner and force you to look through lenses you cannot focus with. This prevents you from fixing your vision on something, which would make it difficult for the doctor to see eye movement abnormalities that might be present.

Hearing Tests

Since the hearing and balance portions of the inner ear are closely related, testing usually begins with a complete evaluation of your hearing. A drop in hearing in either or both ears may provide clues that there is damage to the vestibular system as well. An audiologist may check your hearing before you see the doctor, or your otolaryngologist might have you listen to a tuning fork(s) placed behind your ears or on your forehead. You might be asked to compare sounds or say when a sound disappears. Some of the possible tests are "pure tone air and bone conduction," "speech reception threshold," "speech discrimination," "tympanometry," "acoustic reflex threshold and decay," "rollover," and "otoacoustic emissions."

Electronystagmography Tests

Other tests may further evaluate the relationship between your eyes and your vestibular system. This kind of testing is called electronystagmography (ENG).

For example during a test called the Dix-Hallpike, nystagmus may be observed or recorded by ENG as you are moved from a sitting to a lying position and your head moves backward and to the side.

During another test called the caloric, warm and cold water or air is circulated through a small balloon on the end of a tube in your ear canal. The changing temperature stimulates your vestibular system and causes nystagmus. For this test, areas around your eyes will be cleaned and sticky-patch electrodes applied so that your eye movements can be electrically monitored.

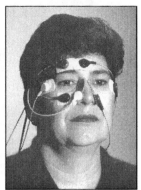

Figure 5-1: Sticky-patch electrodes. Someone is being prepared for ENG testing. (Courtesy of Micromedical Technologies, Chatham, Illinois.)

Rotational Tests

The traditional method of rotation testing involved spinning you on a revolving chair and observing your eye movements. This testing is now performed with a computer-controlled rotation chair programmed to turn gently to the right and left. As the chair rotates, nystagmus is recorded by ENG.

Another kind of rotational test is called the auto-rotational test. It measures your ability to keep your eyes focused on a stationary target during active head movement. This testing is performed with a computer-controlled rotation chair. Electrodes are placed on your face to measure eye movement, and a device resem-

Figure 5-2: Rotary chair. (Courtesy of Micromedical Technologies, Chatham, Illinois.)

bling a band is placed around your head to measure head movement.

In addition to tests in a rotary chair or auto-rotation device, your doctor may perform non-computerized rotational tests by moving your head back and forth and looking for nystagmus.

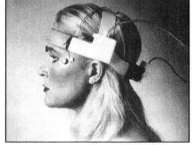

Figure 5-3: Vestibular auto-rotation test (VAT). (Courtesy of Western Systems Research, Pasadena, California.)

Moving Platform Tests

Dix-Hallpike, caloric, and rotation testing check only part of the vestibular system—the vestibulo-ocular reflexes (VOR) or reflexes between your vestibular system (specifically, the horizontal semicircular canals) and eye muscles.

Your ability to maintain bal-ance depends not only on VOR, but also on the relationship between your vestibular system and your muscles and joints (VSR or vestibulo-spinal reflexes).

Moving platform tests (posturography) evaluate all three parts of your balance system—your eyes, your muscles and joints, and your vestibular system—simultaneously.

During these tests you stand on a computer-controlled platform which moves as your body sways. As you try to maintain your balance under various conditions, gauges under the platform record shifts in your body weight.

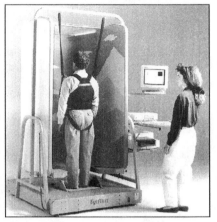

Figure 5-4: Computerized dynamic posturography. (Courtesy of Neuro-Com International, Inc., Clackamas, Oregon.)

Other Tests

Depending on the circumstances, your doctor may also order other kinds of tests, including blood tests, allergy tests, auditory brainstem response (ABR) tests (also known as BER, BSER, and BAER for "brainstem elicited response"), and scans such as magnetic resonance imaging (MRI), computerized tomography (CT or CAT), or X-rays.

Chapter 6

Vestibular Disorders and Disturbances

Once your physician has evaluated all the information from your medical history, examination, and testing, you will be given a diagnosis of your problem. There are many different clinical diagnoses of vestibular disorders. Understanding your specific diagnosis will help you to understand your treatment and rehabilitation process.

Benign Paroxysmal Positional Vertigo (BPPV)

Many dizziness problems turn out to be BPPV, the most common of the vestibular disorders. BPPV is an inner-ear balance disorder characterized by sudden brief bouts of vertigo and nystagmus induced by specific head movements. The two main theories about BPPV suggest that debris floating in a semicircular canal or stuck to the cupula of a canal cause the attacks.

A change of some sort must occur to or in an individual to set BPPV into motion initially. In about half the people with BPPV, this change is never identified. In the other half, one of several things is thought to be the cause. The most common cause of this debris in people under age 50 is thought to be head injury, which may have been either a direct blow to the head or a whiplash injury. The second-leading cause is thought to be change associated with aging. BPPV is much more common in the elderly than in the rest of the population. BPPV is also seen frequently in people with other inner ear conditions such as vestibular neuronitis, Meniere's disease, endolymphatic hydrops, and ototoxicity.

The vertigo of BPPV occurs with head movement and may be accompanied by nausea. The kind of movement that brings on the symptoms is different for each individual, depending on which part of the vestibular system has been affected. Forward-backward movement most commonly causes symptoms. However, moving the head to look upward may cause dizziness for some people, while sudden movement to the left or right may bring on symptoms for others.

Labyrinthitis and Neuronitis

Infections of the inner ear that cause inflammation of the labyrinth (labyrinthitis) or the vestibulo-cochlear nerve (neuronitis) occur infrequently. Viral labyrinthitis, viral neuronitis, and bacterial labyrinthitis can all occur.

Viral labyrinthitis usually causes a sudden, violent onset of vertigo, nausea, vomiting, and sudden hearing loss. Viral neuronitis also causes sudden, violent vertigo, nausea, and vomiting but no hearing loss. Because antibiotics are not effective against viruses, treatment is symptomatic and may include anti-vertiginous medications, antihistamines, and bed rest. Some doctors treat these problems with antiviral drugs. Within a week the person is usually able to sit up and after two weeks will begin to compensate for the dizziness and vertigo. Although permanent vestibular damage may remain in some cases, most people recover fully from viral labyrinthitis.

Bacterial labyrinthitis can occur from the spread of a middle ear infection or brain infection to the inner ear, and on rare occasions it can occur as an adverse effect of middle or inner ear surgery. This kind of infection needs to be treated immediately with antibiotics.

Endolymphatic Hydrops

In the normal inner ear, a sensitive regulation mechanism maintains the composition and pressure of the inner ear fluids (endolymph and perilymph) at constant levels. Although the composition of the blood and other body fluids may vary when we become dehydrated or eat too much salty food, the inner ear fluids remain unchanged.

Occasionally this regulatory system stops working correctly, resulting in too much endolymph in the inner ear. The name for this condition is "endolymphatic hydrops."

The endolymphatic fluid fills the inner ear and bathes the sensory nerve endings of both the hearing and vestibular (balance) structures. As long as the pressure and composition of the fluid remain constant, the nerve endings function normally. However, increased pressure from endolymphatic hydrops can damage any part of the vestibular apparatus or the cochlea.

In most cases the cause of endolymphatic hydrops (or hydrops) is unknown. However, it may occur when a head blow, infection, degeneration of the inner ear, allergy or some other occurrence alters the regulation mechanism of the inner ear. When this happens, fluctuations in blood and other body fluid levels cause fluctuations in the endolymph. Since the sensory nerve endings of the hearing and balance structures are very sensitive to changes in the endolymph surrounding them, they become abnormally stimulated and cause a variety of symptoms.

The symptoms of endolymphatic hydrops may include a feeling of pressure or fullness in the ear, ringing in the ear (tinnitus), hearing loss, dizziness or vertigo (which may be accompanied by nausea and vomiting), and loss of balance.

Meniere's Disease

In 1861 a French physician, Prosper Meniere, described a condition which now bears his name. He was also the first to correctly attribute the cause to the inner ear. Meniere's disease is a disorder of the inner ear that causes these four classic symptoms: vertigo, tinnitus, a feeling of fullness or pressure in the ear, and fluctuating hearing loss.

Meniere's attacks may begin with little warning, or tinnitus or a feeling of ear fullness may precede them. An attack usually lasts for a short time (minutes to hours). An acute attack of Meniere's disease is thought to result from fluctuating pressure of the endolymph or inner ear fluid.

The underlying cause of Meniere's disease is unknown.

The number of people who have Meniere's disease in one ear (unilateral) and who will ultimately develop the problem in both ears (bilateral) is unknown. Estimates range from 17.7 percent to 75 percent. A study conducted in Rochester, Minn., from 1951 to 1980 reported a 34 percent rate of bilateral disease over time.

Hearing fluctuates, and a gradual loss of hearing occurs, depending on the number of episodes. As the disease progresses, the loss of hearing first becomes worse for lower tones, then affects both high and low tones.

Meniere's disease affects about 46 out of 100,000 people. The majority of people affected are more than 40 years old, and recent evidence indicates that Meniere's is slightly more common in women than in men.

Vertebrobasilar Insufficiency

The vertebral and basilar arteries carry blood to the inner ear labyrinth, the vestibulo-cochlear nerve, and the brainstem. When blood flow through these vessels is restricted for any reason, it is called vertebrobasilar insufficiency (VBI). VBI is a common cause of vertigo in the elderly. The vertigo occurs suddenly without warning, usually lasts for several minutes, and is often accompanied by nausea and vomiting. Other symptoms such as headache, hallucinations and impaired vision usually occur during the episodes of vertigo.

In any case where circulation to the inner ear is impaired, the main goal of treatment is to provide sufficient oxygen to the sensory and other cells. Depending on the cause of reduced blood flow, treatment may include steroids to reduce swelling of damaged tissues, oxygen therapy to increase the amount of oxygen the blood is carrying to the inner ear and/or medications to reduce the tendency to form clots which may impede blood flow.

Migraine

Migraine is a disorder usually associated with headache. However, symptoms may also include vertigo and imbalance. Studies indicate that about 25 percent of migraine sufferers experience dizziness during the attacks.

Labyrinthine Concussion

Loss of vestibular function on one side may be the result of head trauma. Either a fracture of the temporal bone, the bone of the skull in which the inner ear is located, or a concussion, a blow to the head that does not cause fracture, may damage the inner ear labyrinth. This is called labyrinthine concussion.

The person who has sustained damage to one side of the vestibular system may experience episodes of nystagmus and vertigo when his or her head position changes. There may also be a sudden loss of hearing. These symptoms may improve over a period of time ranging from a few months to two years. Hearing loss from a labyrinthine concussion is usually permanent.

Perilymph Fistula

A perilymph fistula is an opening or tear in one or both of the small openings (the round window and the oval window) between the middle and inner ears. These windows separate the middle-ear space from the fluid-filled inner ear. A fistula in either or both of these openings allows the inner fluid to leak into the middle-ear space. This leakage disturbs the normal pressure of the inner ear fluid; as a result both balance and hearing may be affected.

Fistulas can exist from birth or result from pressure injuries such as those that sometimes occur during scuba diving, or they may result from direct blows to the head or whiplash. One or both ears may be damaged.

Changes in air pressure that occur in the middle ear (for example, when your ears "pop" in an airplane) normally do not affect your inner ear. But when a fistula is present, changes in air pressure directly affect the inner ear, stimulating the balance and/or hearing structures and causing symptoms.

Typical symptoms of perilymph fistula include dizziness, vertigo, imbalance, nausea, and vomiting. Some people experience ringing or fullness in the ears, and many notice a hearing loss. Most people with fistulas find that their symptoms get worse with changes in altitude (elevators, airplanes, mountain roads) or with exercise.

Cholesteatoma

Tumors may also affect the functioning of the vestibular system. Among these is cholesteatoma, a cyst-like growth that may form as a result of chronic middle ear infection or perforated eardrum. These benign tumors of the middle ear may enlarge and erode into the bone of the inner ear. The symptoms may include hearing loss, vertigo and a foul drainage from the ear.

Cholesteatomas may be removed surgically.

Idiopathic Vestibular Degeneration

Degeneration of the inner ear structures that occurs with no known cause is called idiopathic degeneration. These changes may occur with aging and are commonly associated with balding or graying hair, especially if graying began before age 30. Auditory testing can easily document hearing loss that occurs. But because the loss of vestibular function is gradual and the person may be able to compensate by relying on vision and proprioception, idiopathic vestibular degeneration is more difficult to diagnose.

A common symptom of vestibular degeneration is unsteadiness when walking, especially in a darkened room. Since aging may also result in impaired vision and proprioception, loss of vestibular function is often a contributing factor in dizziness (referred to as multisensory dizziness) in elderly people.

Otic Capsule Softening

Certain autoimmune disorders such as rheumatoid arthritis and lupus erythematosus may cause a softening of the otic capsule, the bone that surrounds the labyrinth of the inner ear. The result may be altered functioning of the vestibular system and dizziness or unsteadiness. When someone's underlying disease is treated successfully, these symptoms may be controlled. In some cases, steroids may also be used to treat otic capsule softening.

Acoustic Neuroma

Acoustic neuroma is a serious but non-cancerous tumor of the vestibulo-cochlear nerve. (This nerve is also referred to as the acoustic nerve, hence the name.) The most common symptoms of acoustic neuroma are progressive hearing loss and tinnitus on one side. Vertigo is a bit unusual. If any vestibular symptoms are present, they're usually in the form of general imbalance or dizziness.

If the tumor is slow growing, a person may be able to compensate for altered vestibular function. However, if the tumor enlarges greatly, other nerves may be affected, causing facial numbness or paralysis. An acoustic neuroma may need to be removed by one or more means.

Ototoxicity

Loss of vestibular function on both sides can result from exposure to poisons, also called ototoxins. These substances can cause temporary or permanent damage to the vestibular parts of the ear and also to the hearing parts. One group of intravenously administered antibiotics, the aminoglycosides, is particularly linked with ototoxicity. When this kind of damage occurs from aminoglycosides, it usually involves both ears and is often permanent.

People who have been exposed to aminoglycosides may experience unsteadiness, loss of hearing, and oscillopsia (bouncing vision). Both vestibular and hearing losses that occur because of aminoglycoside toxicity are usually permanent.

High doses of salicylates or aspirin-containing drugs may cause temporary hearing loss and tinnitus, or rarely may cause dizziness, imbalance or vertigo. These symptoms usually disappear rapidly when the medications are discontinued.

Symptoms Caused by Alcohol

The ingestion of alcohol commonly causes nystagmus and vertigo. Symptoms may begin within a half-hour after drinking the alcohol and may continue past the time that alcohol can be detected in the person's blood. These effects are temporary and will subside. (However, long-term alcohol abuse that damages the cerebellum may cause permanent dizziness, vertigo, and imbalance.)

Central Nervous System Disorders

Certain disorders that affect the brain, cranial nerves, or spinal cord may cause symptoms of dizziness or vertigo. One example is multiple sclerosis, a disease of unknown cause that attacks nerves throughout the body. Vertigo is the first symptom noticed by approximately 10 percent and occurs eventually in half the people diagnosed with multiple sclerosis. Some people with Bell's palsy, a disease of the facial nerve that results in facial paralysis, may also experience dizziness or vertigo if the vestibulo-cochlear nerve is affected.

Chapter 7

Treatment

When you are diagnosed with a balance disorder, your recovery process often depends on how actively you participate in your treatment and rehabilitation. When you understand your diagnosis and the reasons for the treatment and/or therapy your physician suggests, you are better prepared to keep to your treatment schedule. The prospect of improving your situation is better.

Obtaining Information

Ask your doctor to explain clearly what your diagnosis means. Why do your symptoms occur? What causes them? How will the recommended treatment affect your condition? What are the alternatives? What are the risks of the treatment? If you don't understand the explanations, don't be afraid to ask for more information—even diagrams, if you think that might be helpful. Your physician will realize that if you understand your problem, you will be more successful in sticking to your treatment.

Make sure that your physician and pharmacist know about all the drugs you are taking, even those prescribed by another physician or purchased over-the-counter.

Whatever your treatment includes—medication, exercise, vestibular rehabilitation therapy, diet, or surgery—your directions should be outlined in detail. Because you will receive a great deal of information when you talk with your doctor about your diagnosis and treatment, it will help to have a family member or friend with you. Together you can keep track of everything that is said. If you take notes, too, you'll be able to use them to refresh your memory after you leave the doctor's office. If your doctor won't supply you with the information you need, you may need to find another doctor.

Medications

In some cases your physician may prescribe one or more medications as part of your treatment. No drugs have been developed specifically to treat vestibular disorders, but some medications used routinely for other conditions are effective in vestibular cases, too. For vestibular disorders, however, these drugs are used in entirely different dosages and on different schedules. You may have friends with high blood pressure or heart disease who are taking the same medications as you but with different dosages and different schedules. Don't confuse your treatment with theirs.

You should know why each medication is prescribed for you. Be sure you understand the exact directions for taking or for discontinuing each medication. Be aware of possible side effects, and report them to your physician. Observe all suggested precautions.

The medications most commonly used in treatment of inner ear disorders fall into the following six groups:

Anti-motion sickness medications

Anti-motion sickness medications are used first to control your symptoms of dizziness, nausea, lightheadedness, and imbalance. They may include meclizine hydrochloride (Antivert, Bonine, Dramamine Less Drowsy Formula) or dimenhydrinate (Dramamine Original Formula) or diphenhydramine (Benadryl). These medications come in tablet form. It is essential to follow your physician's directions precisely to maintain a consistent level of medication in your bloodstream. Sudden changes in blood levels of these medications may actually increase your symptoms.

Anti-nausea medications

Your doctor may prescribe promethazine (Phenergan) or prochlorperazine (Compazine, Stemetil, Chlorazine) to stop nausea and vomiting. These medications are available in various forms.

Anti-anxiety drugs

Under certain circumstances anti-anxiety medications, the benzodiazepines, may be prescribed. These drugs include diazepam (Valium), alprazolam (Xanax), lorazepam (Ativan), and clonazepam (Klonopin).

Anti-virals

If a virus is thought to be the problem, such as in vestibular neuronitis or Ramsay-Hunt syndrome, anti-viral drugs may be prescribed.

Diuretics

People with endolymphatic hydrops or Meniere's disease are instructed to drink sufficient fluids to replace fluid loss because of exercise, heat, or other causes, to avoid foods containing high amounts of salt or sugar, and to distribute their food and fluid intake evenly throughout each day. In addition they may be given small doses of diuretics to help their kidneys work at a constant rate throughout the day.

When the doctor's instructions are followed precisely, body fluid levels (including the fluid levels in the inner ears) remain stable.

Seesaw fluid levels that adversely affect the function of the inner ear can be minimized.

Hydrochlorothiazide (HCTZ) is a commonly used diuretic.

Because there is a tendency to lose an excessive amount of potassium when certain diuretics are used, a potassium supplement may be prescribed to take with the diuretic. This medication maintains your body fluid potassium at the normal level essential for proper functioning of your heart, muscles, nerves, and other body organs. Some diuretics are combinations of HCTZ and a potassium-sparing drug; examples of these combinations are Maxzide and Dyazide.

Steroids

Sometimes doctors will prescribe a steroid to treat inflammation within the inner ear or to stop an immune reaction. Steroids can be taken orally, in which case they act systemically rather than locally. They can also be given locally by injection through the eardrum into the middle ear space. Dexamethasone (Decadron) is an example of a steroid that has been used in this way.

BPPV Maneuvers

If you have been diagnosed with BPPV, your doctor may prescribe physical maneuvers to treat your condition. The doctor may perform the physical maneuvers (canalith repositioning or liberatory or other) or may refer you to a physical therapist or other health professionals skilled in these treatments. The maneuvers are designed to move debris to non-sensitive places within the inner ear and to do this without risk to hearing or balance.

Referral to Other Services

It's important for you to become actively involved in your own therapy as you recover from a balance disorder. Follow your doctor's recommendations about medications strictly. Be willing to restrict your activity (or possibly increase it) after surgery. If your treatment includes physical therapy, follow your directions faithfully.

Your doctor may make specific recommendations concerning your diet, physical activity, and stress management. You will probably feel that you need to learn more about what you can do to control your symptoms. You'll find many suggestions in the second half of this book. In addition, if you wish, your doctor can refer you to other health professionals for assistance.

Physical therapist

People who have been living with their symptoms of dizziness and imbalance for a long time develop many habits to compensate for their impaired balance systems. They become overly dependent on either vision or on the information from their muscles and joints to maintain their balance. To avoid a resurgence of their symptoms, they have learned to carry out their activities of daily living while avoiding head movement. In many cases, these modifications in posture and movement are responsible for increased stress and fatigue or even increased symptoms.

Physical therapists can identify these compensatory adjustments. If you visit one for treatment of a vestibular disorder, he or she will assess the kinds of balance strategies you use. (Do you always bend at the knees rather than at the hips to pick something up from the floor? Do you rotate at the waist rather than turning your head?)

A therapist can also determine how well you use other senses to help with balance. (Do you rely heavily on vision or touch?) Contributing factors are assessed, too. (Do you have arthritis? Are you normally active or inactive?)

Physical therapists can also teach you relaxation techniques that reduce muscle stress and fatigue. They will develop therapeutic exercise routines that help "teach" your vestibular system to work effectively once again.

If your physician prescribes physical therapy, you may find that the exercises are uncomfortable at first. They may actually provoke episodes of dizziness or vertigo. But with time and consistent repetition, your symptoms will decrease as your brain begins to recognize the input it receives from your vestibular system as "normal." You will gradually be able to increase your physical activities.

The physical therapist's goal for a patient with a balance disorder is to restore the former activity level and to enable the patient's return to work. After completing a prescribed physical therapy program, you will be encouraged to become involved in some kind of physical activity. A life-long exercise program is a good practice in general and more important for people who have balance disorders.

Occupational therapist

Sometimes there are ways you can change your environment or the way you perform certain tasks so that you can avoid provoking a dizziness attack. If you think it might be helpful to get some individualized advice, your doctor may refer you to an occupational therapist.

Occupational therapists analyze your home, your work place, and your recreational activities. They then recommend changes that will allow you to better manage your symptoms and increase your safety.

Dietitian

People with certain balance disorders must control the amounts of salt and sugar in their diets. (See Chapter 10: "Watching What You Eat.")

Dieticians can help you plan a nutritional program to meet your special needs. If you feel that you would benefit from learning more about ways to manage your diet, your doctor may refer you to a dietitian for special assistance.

Psychological counselor

There may be times when you feel completely overwhelmed trying to cope with the problems of living with your balance disorder. If you are affected by chronic symptoms you may feel as though you may never get well. Perhaps your symptoms have been so severe in the past that you avoid leaving your home. You may have become isolated from your friends. The frustration of living with constant dizziness may have made you so irritable that you and your family are constantly at odds.

If these problems are affecting you or your family, you may find it helpful to talk to a psychiatrist, a psychologist or a social worker—someone who is used to working with others who have chronic disorders. They understand the stresses and burdens of coping with the physical, emotional, social, and financial problems that affect people with chronic disorders. Your physician can refer you to a counselor who can help you and your family identify those problems and solve them successfully.

Social worker

Sometimes it's hard for you and your family to cope with all the problems you face. You may need to turn to your community for help—transportation, home maintenance, and financial assistance. The federal, state, county, and other local governments in your area maintain a comprehensive system of social services that may be available to you. Many service organizations provide assistance to those in need.

Contact your local United Way's Information and Referral Office for more information on services that are available in your area. Most services are provided free or at minimal cost. Local Senior Centers usually maintain referral services for older adults. Your physician's office or the patient relations office at your local hospital are other sources for information.

Surgery

For some patients, surgery may be recommended, depending on the extent and location of the inner ear problem. The severity of the patient's symptoms and amount of hearing loss are always carefully assessed before a decision to perform surgery is made. Surgical procedures include such things as gentamicin treatment, posterior canal plugging, acoustic neuroma removal, perilymph fistula repair, endolymphatic shunt, and vestibular nerve section.

In some cases the symptoms that a patient experiences immediately after surgery may seem worse than they were before. A gradual recovery from dizziness symptoms occurs over a period of time with follow-up treatment.

Your physical activities may be greatly restricted following surgery, or you may be required to begin an exercise schedule immediately in order to rehabilitate your balance system. This will depend on the type of surgery you have had.

Whenever you and your physician are considering surgery, you should discuss the following questions:

• How will the surgery improve my condition?
• Will my symptoms disappear immediately?
• Might my symptoms seem worse following surgery?
• If my condition is degenerative, will the surgery help or will my condition keep deteriorating?
• What are the risks of this surgery?
• Will my hearing be affected?
• Can my problem be transferred to the other ear as a result of surgery?
• What are the chances of success?
• What is the ratio of success for this procedure?
• If the surgery is not successful, will my symptoms be worse than they are now?
• What will the procedure entail?
• Will the incision be made inside my ear or behind my ear?
• How long does it usually take?
• How long do you anticipate that I will be hospitalized?
• When will I be able to return to work?

Chapter 8

Insurance

T esting, diagnosis, and treatment for your dizziness and balance disorder are usually covered by your health insurance. Because some of the diagnoses of specific disorders may be unfamiliar to certain insurance companies, your physician may provide a written explanation outlining your diagnosis in some detail to the insurance company.

Health Insurance

Health insurance comes in many varieties and with a staggering number of rules and regulations. It can be divided generally into traditional insurance coverage, PPOs, HMOs, Medicaid, and Medicare. The information below will give you an overview of health insurance. Refer to your insurance policy for any specific information you may need about benefits, rules, and regulations.

PPO Health Insurance

Preferred provider organization (PPO) health insurance usually allows you to visit any doctor in any place, but your out-of-pocket expense will be lower if you choose someone on the PPO's list of preferred providers. The list generally includes doctors, hospitals, labs, radiology offices, pharmacies, and other health-care professionals and agencies.

A typical arrangement is for the PPO to pay 90 percent and for you to pay 10 percent of the bills for treatment by a preferred provider. If you choose a non-preferred provider for treatment, the PPO will pay less, and you will pay more.

HMO Health Insurance

Insurance from a health maintenance organization (HMO) involves a membership contract between you and the organization. By joining, you are allowing the HMO to decide what health care you will receive and from whom. If you want the HMO to pay for your medical bills, your choice is limited to those providers, facilities, and hospitals under contract with that particular HMO. Your bills will not be paid if you seek care outside of the HMO while you are living at home. Different rules apply when you are traveling.

Traditional Health Insurance

With traditional health insurance, you pay a monthly premium, and the insurance company pays a percentage of your medical bills. The percentage the insurance company pays is determined by the individual policy. Usually you are responsible for the first $250 to $500 of charges (the deductible) each year. After the deductible limit is reached, the insurer will usually pay 80 percent of a "reasonable and customary" charge as defined by the insurance company, and you will pay 20 percent. With this kind of policy, the insurer places no restrictions on which doctor you see. Generally, this type of health insurance is the most expensive, and it is the least likely to be available from your employer.

Medicare

Medicare is a kind of U.S. Federal health insurance available to people receiving Social Security retirement benefits or Social Security disability benefits.

People are automatically eligible for Medicare after receiving Social Security disability benefits for two years. Enrollment in Medicare decreases the monthly disability check by the relatively small cost of the Medicare premium.

Medicare coverage includes various options, including using an HMO. Get and read current Medicare publications before making any decisions about health insurance coverage. Keep in mind that if you don't enroll for Medicare when it is first offered to you, you will pay a much higher premium if you enroll later.

Medicaid

Medicaid is a kind of governmental health insurance for the indigent. Both the U.S. Federal government and individual state governments fund this insurance. Because of this setup, Medicaid eligibility and benefits can differ significantly from state to state.

Generally, to qualify for Medicaid your monthly income must be very low and your bank accounts must be very small.

Common Health Insurance Terms

Authorization, pre-authorization, or *referral* are terms used by insurers to mean the process of granting official permission to see a specialist or have a test or procedure done that can't be done by your primary care doctor. This permission may be given verbally or in writing. Different health plans have different rules; ask about them when you are told to go for specialty care or testing. It's always best to get this permission in writing and to double-check its validity with the insurance company.

Pre-certification is another term used to mean the process of getting official permission from your insurance company for something such as an MRI (or other equally expensive test) or surgery. Pre-certification has become routine with most insurers, including Medicare, Medicaid, PPOs, and traditional health insurers.

A *co-payment* or *co-insurance* refers to a fixed amount of money you pay for a visit to the doctor's office, usually $10 to $15, in addition to the money paid for the visit by your insurance.

A *deductible* is the total amount of money you must spend on your annual health care bills before your insurance company begins to pay. Only health care covered by your insurance policy counts toward the total.

In-patient and *outpatient* are important terms because some insurance companies pay at one rate for outpatient tests and procedures and at another rate for in-patient. These two terms have blurred significantly over the last several years. Staying overnight in the hospital used to define the difference; now you may be considered an outpatient even if your hospital stay is as much as 23 hours and includes one night.

Medically necessary is a term used to describe whether or not your insurance company considers a test, office visit, procedure, or treatment necessary given your diagnosis and condition. Whether or not your primary doctor or specialist thinks it is needed is not the question.

Insurers use *usual and customary, usual and prevailing,* or *allowable* to mean what, in their view, something should cost. This is not necessarily what your doctor charges or what anyone else has charged you.

Privacy

Insurance companies almost always insist upon having full access to your medical records as a pre-requisite to paying your claim. In many cases, you will be asked to sign a form giving your doctor permission to send any requested part of your medical record to your insurance company. The only way you can avoid this loss of privacy is to pay for your own care.

COBRA

If you are unable to perform your job and leave work of your own accord or you are fired, you may be eligible to maintain your employee health insurance policy through the Consolidated Omnibus Budget Reconciliation Act of 1985 (COBRA). This Federal law requires any employer with 20 or more employees to offer continued health insurance after an employee has left a job. The coverage must usually be provided for 18 months, possibly more under certain circumstances. This act does not require the employer to pay for the coverage, only to provide the departing employee with the opportunity to buy it. In order to qualify, you must sign up within 60 days of leaving your job.

Disability Insurance

Only a small number of people with a diagnosed vestibular problem will become too disabled to continue working for pay. According to the 1995 annual report of the National Institute on Deafness and Other Communication Disorders, during 1994 only an estimated 7,600 people throughout the U.S. received Social Security benefits (Social Security Disability Insurance payments and Supplemental Security Income payments combined) for balance problems.

Note about working: Try to continue working if you can, safely. Usually, Social Security disability payments and private disability insurance will not come close to matching your normal paycheck. Also, even if you qualify for Social Security disability, you will not be eligible for health insurance from Medicare until two years later.

Disability benefits may be available from a private insurance policy and/or the government via the Social Security Administration for people unable to keep their jobs.

Benefits from private policies differ from situation to situation. Most policies have a choice of elimination periods (the varying periods of time that must go by before certain benefits begin) and different amounts of payment. These policies are usually set up to cover you for a short time until you qualify for Social Security disability benefits.

If you did not buy a private disability insurance policy on your own, check to see if you have such coverage through your employer. (Sometimes such coverage is referred to as "short term disability.")

Social Security Disability

The Social Security Administration oversees two different programs related to disability, Social Security Disability Insurance (SSDI) and Supplemental Security Income (SSI). The same process for each program determines a person's disability, but the financial eligibility differs. Financial eligibility for SSDI payments is based on how much you have contributed to Social Security over time. On the other hand,

SSI payments are made on the basis of your current financial need, and your past contributions to Social Security are not taken into account.

For information about Social Security programs, visit your local Social Security office or call 1-800-772-1213. Hearing-impaired callers using TTY equipment can reach Social Security between 7 a.m. and 7 p.m. weekdays by calling 1-800-325-0778. To view Social Security information on the Internet, go to www.ssa.gov.

Chapter 9

Helping Yourself

Managing Acute Attacks

Bouts of intense symptoms from Meniere's disease and other vestibular disorders may occur and may last for varying lengths of time. These attacks may be quite disabling. Here are some actions you can take to minimize your symptoms.

If you feel symptoms coming on and have previously discussed symptom-blocking drugs with your physician, take your drugs before the symptoms are totally upon you. Then immobilize your head. The best place to be is on the floor. Even a bed or couch may afford too much movement. Then, without moving your head, you should fix your eyes on something stable.

Secondly, do not move until your nausea subsides. Then, first move your eyes, then your arms and legs, and gradually add more movement until you feel your condition improving. These movements should be attempted without changing the position of your head or what you are looking at.

Let yourself throw up if you have to. When you become thirsty, gradually try small sips of water or other fluids if you can tolerate them. If your vestibular disorder has previously been diagnosed, you may take medications that have been prescribed to relieve the symptoms. If you couldn't take prescribed drugs before the attack, take them now.

Following an acute attack, try to sleep.

Finally, even if you feel better following an acute attack, avoid high-risk activities such as going up or down stairs, moving around in a dark room or driving, usually for the rest of the day.

Reducing Stress

Changing your lifestyle to minimize stress, both in your daily activities and in your relationships with others, may be the most difficult part of learning to live with dizziness. How often do you hear "slow down, take your time"? Continuing at top speed is impossible for a person experiencing dizziness. When stress begins to overwhelm you, it's time to make some changes.

First of all, learn to recognize your symptoms of stress. Do you have some early warning signals? Does your head begin to ache? Do you feel tension in your neck muscles or your shoulders? Listen to what your body is telling you. By heeding these signals, you can recognize that stress is beginning to affect you.

Next, identify the source or sources of your stress. Does the thought of leaving your home and going out alone panic you? Perhaps your greatest frustration arises when you become confused and are unable to read or to remember the words you want to use during a conversation. Having to give up some of your favorite activities and knowing that other people don't understand how you feel is distressing, too.

Finally, take action to change these stressful situations.

Your first step should be to establish good communication patterns. Don't be afraid to ask for what you need or want. Explain to your family and friends that you have a problem and indicate specifically what they can do to help you.

Involving Your Family

Because you usually don't look sick, even when you feel miserable, it's important to let others, especially your family, know how you feel. Susan Lee, who has BPPV, experienced a few very distressing days following her discharge from the hospital until she and her family agreed to some changes that would make her feel more comfortable.

Susan's most uncomfortable moments came at dinner. Seated at the large dining room table in the midst of her four brothers and sisters and her parents, she felt overwhelmed by the noisy chatter and swirl of activity surrounding her. Everyone seemed to talk at once, with hands waving, and dishes being passed back and forth. Susan spent most mealtimes staring at the floor, barely touching her food, and trying to shut out the confusion. By the time dinner was over each night, she felt tense and nauseated and totally frustrated.

Susan finally asked that some changes be made. Dinner was served in the dining room, where the lights could be dimmed slightly, and the carpeting absorbed some of the noise. She was given a seat at the end of the table so that she could see all the family members without having to turn her head constantly from side to side. Conversation never lagged, but everyone attempted to speak in turn and tried to keep general activity a little more subdued. The family agreed that these changes were a small price to pay to have Susan included comfortably during mealtimes again.

A dizziness or balance disorder may change a person's family role significantly. He may be unable to help with housework or go to baseball practice after a long day at work. She may be unable to hold a full-time job.

Your family may become over-protective. Your spouse may assume that you are unable to cope with certain situations.

Joan Adams, who has Meniere's disease, discovered that when she told her family how she was feeling, they could help her through the times when she felt dizzy and was unable to participate in family activities.

"Because I had been affected by episodes of severe dizziness for many years, my family was used to having me refuse invitations to dinner and other social occasions with our friends," said Joan. "I found out that there were often times when my husband was turning down invitations for me, assuming that I wouldn't feel up to going out. I really resented that."

Every time Joan had experienced an acute episode of dizziness because of her Meniere's disease, she made every effort to avoid missing work and to make sure that the household ran smoothly. The strain of trying to maintain her usual schedule was making her tense and irritable.

Joan decided that she needed to be honest with her family. When she finally explained how she felt, her family began to understand. Now everyone shares the household responsibilities so that Joan can take some time out when she needs to, and her husband, realizing that Joan needs to get out and relax with friends when she feels up to it, checks with her before he accepts or declines an invitation.

In some cases, it may be very difficult for you or your family to accept the fact that changes must be made. Your children may feel angry that Mom or Dad can't play tennis with them anymore.

Your spouse may feel that he or she is being expected to shoulder too large a burden of job, housekeeping, and raising children practically alone.

Changes in role or responsibilities within your family must be clearly communicated. You need to let your family members know what you want to do and what you are capable of doing. Being open and honest about how you feel and what your limitations are will lead to better understanding within your family.

Being Honest with Friends

Because you have no outward signs of your disorder—no cast on your leg or scar from your surgery—it may be difficult for friends to realize that you have a physical problem. There have probably been times when you found it necessary to cancel activities at the last minute. Because you "looked good" they may not have realized how miserable you felt.

Friends may refrain from asking you to participate in an activity just because you have sometimes had to cancel similar plans in the past. You need to make it clear to them exactly what aggravates your symptoms. Tell them that your dizziness episodes may occur period-ically. Let them know that you wish to continue to participate as often as you can. It is important that you seek out activities that make you feel needed, and that you know someone is depending on you to accomplish a needed task.

Community involvement had always been an important part of Anne White's life. When she began to experience periodic dizziness episodes, she was forced to drop out of many volunteer activities.

"I had always been active as a volunteer in my son's pre-school. But when I began to experience frequent attacks of dizziness, there were times that I had to cancel activities at the last minute," said Anne. "Pretty soon I realized that the school had stopped calling me. I guess they assumed that I was unreliable. Timmy was really disap-pointed, too.

"I decided to meet with the volunteer chairperson to explain my situation. She was very understanding, and as a result, she has begun to call on me again. We have worked out an arrangement so that I always volunteer with someone who can back me up in case of an emergency. I really enjoy being able to participate, and it's nice to know that I can help."

Make a real effort to avoid becoming isolated from your friends. When you are experiencing severe dizziness, you may have to turn down invitations. But as your symptoms diminish, gradually increase your social contacts again. Invite one or two friends to visit you in your home at first. In familiar surroundings there are fewer outside distractions and less confusion. You will feel more secure and can enjoy your friends more comfortably.

Staying Active

If affected by dizziness or a balance disorder, you may feel worse when you are physically active. You probably tend to avoid any move-ment, especially head movement, as much as possible.

If you make the effort to remain active, you may well end up feeling better. You will have more energy and get tired less often. Staying active helps you manage your symptoms of dizziness and imbalance.

Before embarking on any exercise program, be sure to check with your physician. There may be times—following surgery, for instance—that any physical activity would actually be detrimental to your recovery.

Increasing activity gradually

One of the best ways to begin managing your symptoms is to get into the best physical condition that you can. This not only means maintaining your ideal weight but also exercising on a regular basis.

An essential part of your recovery is a gradual increase in physical exercise and a reintroduction to activities that cause your symptoms of dizziness and imbalance. Repeating the movements that cause your dizziness allows your brain to adjust to the input it receives. With time, your brain "reads" this input as normal and your symptoms begin to subside.

Karen Cooper is an example of someone who, with consistent exercise, succeeded in retraining her balance system.

Karen's severe attacks of vertigo had confined her to her apartment for several months before a scheduled vestibular surgery. Immediately after surgery, her symptoms seemed worse than ever. The room whirled around her. She clutched the sides of the mattress to keep from being thrown off the bed. She was sure that the surgery had been a big mistake. Now here was Dr. Johnson standing over her saying, "I want you to sit up, Karen. You have to be ready to take a walk down the hallway tomorrow." "Walk down the hall?" thought Karen. "I'll be lucky if I can ever stand up again."

The next morning Karen clung desperately to the wall as she slowly made her way about 20 feet down the corridor. Each day the distance increased. Soon after her release from the hospital she was walking outdoors, first around the block, then for a mile or two. Within ten weeks she was jogging, and after eight months she began an exercise class that she continues to attend four to five times a week.

Avoiding fatigue

It is also important to prevent over-exertion or fatigue. You may need to schedule some time each day for a rest period. After a while you will notice when you are beginning to feel tired, and that's the time to stop.

Sue Walsh, a schoolteacher with BPPV, knows exactly what she needs to do. "After a hectic day at work, I find that a short nap as soon as I get home refreshes me. It gives me the energy I need to participate in an aerobics class three nights each week."

Precautions

Your physician or physical therapist will develop some of the exercises that you do as a specific part of your treatment. These exercises often cause dizziness or imbalance at first.

During your daily activities, there are some precautions you can take to prevent dizziness. When you get out of bed, don't roll over or stand up quickly. Turn on your side, swing your legs over the side, and slowly sit up on the edge of the bed. When you stand up, ease yourself up slowly, holding on to the arm of a chair or other support until you are stable.

When you put on shoes or stockings, sit down and raise your foot up rather than bending over. Try to avoid bending your head back quickly, as you might when looking up at a high shelf. Any rapid motions, such as snapping your head around in response to "Oh, look at this," may also bring on dizziness. You might ask your friends to try not to startle you.

Women should avoid high-heeled shoes because they allow minimum contact with the surface they are standing on. Flat, non-skid shoes provide you with a more stable base and better input from your feet to your brain. Many companies produce "walking" shoes well-suited to maintaining balance. When you are feeling dizzy, you are more dependent on your sense of touch to maintain your balance. You may want to use a cane, some other support object, or have another person walk with you.

Try new activities in familiar surroundings where you feel most secure and comfortable. When you decide to take a walk outdoors, try it first in front of your own house, and allow a family member or friend to assist you. Looking at the ground while you are walking may be helpful at first. Before attempting dinner in a restaurant, invite one or two close friends to your home for an evening. Gradually expose yourself to increased noise, confusion, and activity.

As your activity level increases, be alert to subtle changes in your general physical condition or in your symptoms. You may become aware that there are certain situations or activities that initiate your dizziness. If this is the case, you may be able to predict when an attack is imminent and take measures to protect yourself or avoid it.

Preparing for Ups and Downs

Recognize that other physical changes may also affect your balance system. Fatigue, monthly hormone fluctuations in women, minor illnesses, allergies, and changes in physical disorders such as diabetes or thyroid dysfunction may aggravate your dizziness symptoms at times. Be aware that these alterations in balance function are temporary and your condition will stabilize when your hay fever, diabetes, or other problem is under control.

Recovery from an inner ear disorder is a slow, gradual process. At times, your symptoms may seem to recur or get worse. You may have occasional setbacks. Knowing that this is not uncommon may help you through some difficult times.

Thinking Positively

Remember that your condition may change frequently. Just

because you weren't able to cope with the confusing activity in a large shopping center a few months ago doesn't mean that you can't handle it now.

Thinking that you can do it is the first step.

Chapter 10

Watching What You Eat

Managing your dizziness and imbalance may mean being told to change your eating habits. "Horrors!" you say. "Give up popcorn at the movies? No more blueberry blintzes for Sunday brunch? How can I enjoy life without chocolate?"

Well, it's not that bad. Most people who stick to a few basic guidelines find that they (and their families) not only eat better but also feel better. They make better choices of what to eat and when to eat.

Balanced Diet

"A balanced diet, in moderate amounts, at regular intervals" is sound advice. Skipping breakfast and lunch, then over-eating during a late evening meal, is dreadful nutritional practice for anyone. For some people with balance disorders, it is disastrous. See-saw levels of salts and sugars in your body fluids may disturb the regulation of your inner ear fluids and provoke dizziness. To avoid that, keep your intake of food and liquids spread evenly throughout the day.

You can help control your symptoms by being aware of foods that seem to bring on episodes of dizziness. You may want to keep a daily journal for a while. Soon you'll be able to identify the kinds of foods that affect you most.

You may also find that your eating patterns will change when you begin to pay attention to what you put in your mouth. You and your family will be eating more nutritious, well-balanced meals.

Less Salt

People with certain balance disorders, such as Meniere's disease or endolymphatic hydrops, must be particularly careful about the amount of salt that they eat. Devouring quantities of pretzels and peanuts can result in almost instant dizziness.

Subjecting your body to a big salt load changes the composition of your body fluids. In some people with Meniere's disease or hydrops, high salt intake affects the inner ear fluids and brings on symptoms.

Table salt is composed of two different elements. It is 40 percent sodium and 60 percent chloride. It's the sodium that causes all the problems. Sodium occurs naturally in foods and drinking water. You can't avoid it. Indeed, you can't live without it. It's an essential ingredient of all body fluids and needed for proper functioning of muscles and nerves.

The minimum daily requirement for one person is 500 mg of sodium—about one-quarter teaspoon of salt. The typical American diet includes 4,000 to 6,000 mg of sodium daily. The American Heart Association recommends staying below 2,400 mg.

If your specific disorder requires that you be on a restricted sodium diet, you will probably be limited to 2,000 mg of sodium per day. That doesn't mean that you can measure out a teaspoonful of salt each morning and sprinkle it with wild abandon throughout the day. Remember that sodium occurs naturally in almost everything you eat. So you must learn to keep score for your sodium intake.

There are lots of places to find information about low salt diets. The American Heart Association is a good source (see www.americanheart.org). Also, VEDA publishes a helpful document called "Dietary Considerations with Secondary Endolymphatic Hydrops, Meniere's Disease, and Vestibular Migraine" (see www.vestibular.org).

Within each of the food groups there are good and bad choices. Fresh or frozen vegetables contain about 35 mg of sodium per half-cup serving, while canned vegetables contain about 150 mg per half-cup. Fresh meat, poultry, or fish have about 75 mg of sodium per ounce. Cured meats such as bacon, hot dogs, and bologna contain more than 10 times as much—750 to 1,000 mg per ounce. A serving of milk or of a natural cheese such as Swiss or cheddar has about 125-150 mg of sodium. Processed cheeses (Parmesan, for example) and cottage cheese have up to 450 mg per serving.

It's important to become an expert label reader. Only one-fourth of the sodium in the average American diet comes from the salt shaker. Most of the other three-quarters comes from processed foods. Many times it is hidden in the form of sodium derivatives used to preserve the food and extend its shelf life. For instance, sodium benzoate is a preservative used in canned vegetables and olives, sodium propionate inhibits mold growth in packaged baked goods, quick-cook cereals are high in disodium phosphate, and ice cream contains sodium alginate to help preserve its texture.

Don't despair. Manufacturers are well aware that many people are concerned about dietary sodium, so low-salt and salt-free grocery items are becoming easier to find on supermarket shelves.

"Sometimes I'm just too tired to think about cooking when I get home from work," says Ruth Andersen, a registered nurse who has

Meniere's disease. "So I always try to keep a supply of low-salt tuna, unsalted peanut butter, and a few other basic low-sodium items on hand. I know there's something easy that I can fix for dinner on those days without having to worry about my salt intake."

Ruth has also learned that it isn't always necessary to purchase the more expensive low sodium grocery items. She uses fresh fruits and vegetables rather than canned ones, or she pours off the liquid and rinses the canned vegetables before cooking. This eliminates one-third to one-half of the salt from the processed food.

If you find that salt-free food is a little too bland for your taste, try experimenting with different herbs and spices. Some favorites include dill on cooked carrots, rosemary with green beans, and lemon juice on just about any vegetable. Use basil, chives, or dry mustard on eggs, and season soups with fresh vegetables, bay leaf and cloves. The possibilities are endless, but for anyone who isn't quite so adventurous, several commercial salt-free seasoning mixes are available. Check your grocer's shelves.

Decreasing the amount of salt in your diet can be an interesting learning process. As you become aware of which foods to avoid, and as the amount of salt in your diet decreases, your desire for salt disappears. In fact, salty foods become unappetizing. And you will be enjoying foods that keep your system in balance.

Note: Check with your physician if you plan to use a salt substitute. Many of these products contain high levels of potassium, which may interfere with certain medications you may be taking.

Less Caffeine

Caffeine can affect the inner ear, resulting in increased symptoms of imbalance and tinnitus (ringing in the ears). It is a chemical that can cause several effects including water loss (diuresis), nervous stimulation, and blood vessel enlargement. All of these can cause dizziness and/or tinnitus in some people.

Coffee and tea contain caffeine, which is also found in most cola drinks and chocolate products, as well as in some over-the-counter medicines. Get used to reading labels, and look for products that are caffeine-free.

Adequate Fluids

Many people with inner ear disorders experience their symptoms if, as a result of dehydration, their inner ear fluids change. Severe dehydration as a result of exercise, hot weather, low fluid intake, or a fever can cause dizziness. To avoid becoming dehydrated, drink adequate amounts of water throughout the day. Many physicians recommend at least eight full glasses of liquids. Try to anticipate body fluid losses that might occur during exercise or hot weather, and be sure to drink extra fluids before you begin exercise.

Ideal Weight

Maintaining your ideal weight is important, too. During episodes of dizziness, you depend more than ever on your sense of touch or proprioception. An extra 20 pounds throws off your center of gravity and makes it more difficult for your muscles to keep your balance.

Little or No Alcohol

Alcohol moves quickly from stomach to bloodstream to endolymphatic fluid of the inner ear, where it interferes with the function of the vestibular system. This may cause dizziness even in people with normal inner ears, and most people with balance disorders are much more sensitive to alcohol's effects. Many people find that limiting or eliminating alcohol helps in symptom control.

Sweets for the Wise

For people with certain vestibular problems, too much sugar can have the same effect as too much salt. High sugar levels in the blood and other body fluids lead to altered composition of the inner ear fluids.

Sugars come in two forms. Complex sugars (or carbohydrates) make up about 22 percent of the food Americans eat. These include starches, grains, beans, peas, and other vegetables. Simple sugars account for 24 percent of our food intake. Table sugar, brown sugar, honey, molasses, and corn syrup are all simple sugars.

Simple sugars are readily broken down in the digestive system and rapidly enter the bloodstream. This means that the sugars from a candy bar or a slice of chocolate cake create a high blood sugar level almost instantly. Then, as the sugar is used by the body for energy, the level drops quickly. In people with hydrops, this fluctuating level of sugar in the body fluids may cause changes in inner ear fluids and result in increased dizziness or other symptoms.

Complex sugars, on the other hand, are digested more slowly. As they are broken down into simple sugars, there is a gradual release of the simple sugar molecules into the bloodstream. Because the body uses these sugars as they become available, there is no rapid rise or fall in blood sugar level. Therefore the inner ear is not as likely to be affected.

Sugars are necessary for proper body function. However, to avoid sugar overload, you should increase the amount of complex sugars you consume while decreasing your intake of simple sugars. In other words, eat more whole grains, beans and vegetables, and stay away from candy and cake. Try to reach the ideal levels recommended by the Nutrition Institute of 43 percent complex sugars and 10 percent simple sugars.

Saccharin, Equal, Sugar Twin, and Nutra-Sweet may be used as sugar substitutes. Nutra-Sweet is sweeter than sugar and has no bitter aftertaste. Nutra-Sweet or Equal may also be used for cooking if the food is prepared at a low temperature for a short time period. Cooking for long periods at high temperatures alters the sugar substitutes and makes them taste bitter.

Here are some "sugarless tips" from a dietitian who works with people who have vestibular disorders.

- Get in the habit of having fruit for dessert instead of pie, cake, cookies, or ice cream.
- Caramelize the sugar naturally present in fruits (bananas, grapefruit) to make them taste sweeter by putting them under the broiler.
- Select fresh fruit or fruits packed in natural juices rather than those packed in heavy syrup.
- Make your own fruit-flavored yogurt. Add fresh fruit to plain yogurt rather than using commercial fruit yogurt, which may contain up to 11 teaspoons of sugar per cup.
- If you are going to have cake, pie, or cookies, make your own and cut the sugar in the recipe by a third or more.
- Sweet breads such as cranberry-nut or raisin-apple make good desserts. They contain relatively little sugar.
- Skip layer cakes that need rich fillings or frostings.
- To make a cake look festive without frosting, place a paper doily over the surface and sprinkle with confectioner's sugar. The pattern will remain when you lift the doily.
- Use naturally sweet eating apples such as golden delicious for baking. You can leave out half of the sugar the recipe calls for.
- Have sugar-free club soda, seltzer, or mineral water mixed with unsweetened fruit juices over ice instead of highly sugared carbonated beverages.
- Try naturally-sweetened, all-fruit jams with no added sugars or sugar substitutes.
- Buy juices with no added sugars, corn syrup, or other sweeteners.
- Herbal teas such as Sweet Almond, Mandarin Orange Spice, and Jasmine are naturally sweet and need little or no sugar.
- If you do drink tea or coffee and use sugar in it, try gradually reducing the amount of sugar you add. It's amazing how quickly you'll learn to enjoy less sweet beverages.

Dining Out

Will your dietary restrictions prevent you from eating out? Absolutely not! The American Heart Association has published information to help guide you through the dining-out dilemma. Call or visit your local chapter, or visit the association's web site at http://www.americanheart.org.

It helps to do some advanced planning, as Jean Johnson has learned. After Jean was diagnosed with endolymphatic hydrops, she wholeheartedly plunged into the task of modifying the way she cooked, altering recipes to fit into her new diet, and paying strict attention to the amounts of salt and sugar she ate. But she and Will, her husband who had recently retired from his job, were very involved in volunteer activities and it wasn't always convenient to eat at home. So Jean decided to talk to the chef at their favorite restaurant.

"Restaurants want your business," Jacques told her. "If you request that your food be prepared without sugar, salt, or sauces, in most cases they will be willing to accommodate you."

It will help if you contact the restaurant in advance. When you call, ask about the food and find out if special requests will be honored. Once you're in the restaurant, be assertive. Remember that you are the patron. Ask your waiter or waitress for advice. And if your food arrives and has not been prepared as you requested, send it back.

If you are on a low-sodium diet, selecting foods that are prepared to order is especially important. Foods prepared in advance often contain salt and MSG (monosodium glutamate) as a preservative. Many Chinese and other Asian preparations contain MSG too. It may be wise to enjoy these foods at home, where you can control the amount of MSG, soy sauce, or salt, or to find restaurants that don't use MSG.

Chapter 11

Getting Organized

Many activities at home and at work require bending, reaching, and turning movements that can aggravate your dizziness symptoms. Be your own efficiency expert. By analyzing and reorganizing the tasks that most frequently cause you discomfort, you can minimize your symptoms and maximize results. Also talk with your M.D. about these things. Your doctor might want you to practice things that can cause you discomfort in order to get you beyond them. Don't restrict your activities without your doctor's input.

Safety First

Your first priority in reorganization should be safety. Remember that you need your sense of touch to help maintain your balance, especially in the dark or if your visual references are moving. Take a close look at the floors in your home and work place. If you have a choice, low pile carpeting or uncovered hard surfaces provide better footing than shag rugs. Throw out the scatter rugs before they throw you. Highly polished floors may be slippery, too, so keep wax to a minimum and be cautious.

Do you have small children at home? Toys on the floor can be dangerous. So can electrical cords, newspapers, and shoes. Alert your family members to the importance of keeping floors free of unnecessary obstructions.

You also depend on vision to help maintain your balance. Good lighting in your home and work place is essential. Dimly lit hallways and dark porches can be obstacle courses for people with balance disorders. Use night lights, too; maintaining a clear, lighted path to the bathroom will help prevent accidents.

Be careful when carrying large cartons, sacks of groceries or other objects that may obstruct your view. It's important to be able to see where your feet are going.

Stairways without railings may prove to be your downfall. All stairways in your home should have strong secure handrails. Some people with balance problems find that the only way they can descend an open stairway is to sit on the steps and "bump" their way down. If you encounter an open stairway without handrails outside your home, don't be afraid to ask for assistance. Play it safe.

Personal Care

Something as simple as changing the way you brush your hair can help eliminate some of your dizziness episodes. Your mother may have taught you that 100 strokes every night would result in thick, shiny tresses. So you throw your head back, then forward, and brush away faithfully every night. Using arm motion instead of vigorous head and neck motion may eliminate a problem with dizziness.

When you shampoo your hair, use a "tearless" shampoo and keep your eyes open for better balance. A proper shower chair might be a good idea. A spray hose attached to the showerhead could make it easier to rinse your hair without bending over.

Placing a rubber mat or installing a non-skid surface on the floor of your shower or bathtub will provide more secure footing for you while you are bathing. A slippery bathtub is an accident waiting to happen. If you or anyone in your family uses bath oil, be sure it's scrubbed out of the tub after every bath.

If you experience severe dizziness symptoms, you may feel more secure if you can be seated while you are bathing. Try a shower stool with rubber suction tips on the legs.

If you are prone to sudden severe attacks of dizziness, nausea and vomiting, you may want to keep unused kitchen trash bags in your car, desk, or briefcase and place a basin or unused trash bag under your bed for nighttime emergencies.

In the Kitchen

Cooking a meal sounds simple enough, but when you begin to analyze all the movement associated with preparation and serving, it's easy to understand why it provokes dizziness for many people who have balance disorders.

You bend over to get pans and mixing bowls from lower cupboards. You look upward and reach for dry ingredients. You walk to the refrigerator and bend down to get the vegetables. You look up to find the glasses. You bend over to put the casserole in the oven. Is it any wonder your symptoms get worse?

Joe Grant, who has BPPV, noticed that cooking in his kitchen required a lot of excess motion—especially head movement that made him dizzy. He found some things he could change.

"I always enjoyed cooking," said Joe. "It was relaxing and gave me an opportunity to be creative. After my accident I found I couldn't look up without becoming dizzy. I had always kept my pots and pans on a high rack above the stove, but I reorganized the kitchen and placed the pans at eye level. Now I don't have to look up and reach so often. Most of my dizziness has disappeared while I'm working in the kitchen, and I can enjoy one of my favorite pastimes again."

Analyze the steps you take while you are fixing dinner. Move the items you use frequently to locations where you can reach them without excessive upward, downward, or turning movements of your head. You'll save time, but more importantly, you'll be able to minimize dizziness symptoms and make meal preparation more enjoyable.

House Cleaning

"No, I don't do windows," said Marilyn. "But I've learned how to keep my dizziness symptoms under control while I get a lot of the other housekeeping chores done."

The frequent up-and-down, side-to-side motions involved in window washing causes dizziness in many people with balance disorders. The same thing is true of painting, so these may be the kinds of activities you'd choose to avoid.

There are ways to handle other housekeeping chores that will allow you to minimize your dizziness and still be able to get the job done. Avoid repetitive back-and-forth or up-and-down head movements while you are dusting, vacuuming, or ironing. Use a broom and a long handled dustpan to clean up crumbs. Wipe up spills with a sponge mop instead of bending over to use a sponge or rag on the floor. If you are sensitive to sound or if noise increases your vestibular symptoms, try wearing anti-noise ear plugs or ear muffs during housecleaning. (Gun stores often carry a wide assortment of excellent anti-noise equipment.) Again, analyze your tasks and observe what activities cause you discomfort. Then, try to find a way to eliminate the movements that provoke your symptoms.

At Work

Your job or your work place should be evaluated carefully for potential problems. Some of these problems can be solved so that you can perform your job efficiently and control your dizziness symptoms. Others may be unavoidable; for safety, you may need to consider a job change.

When operating power equipment is part of your everyday activity at work, you will need to consider the possibility of injury. If you experience dizziness symptoms while you are on the job, you may be putting yourself or others at risk.

Perhaps your job requires a critical need for either balance or hearing function. If working on ladders, scaffolding, or other narrow support surfaces in high places is part of your daily routine, a job change may be necessary for your own safety.

High noise levels aggravate dizziness symptoms for some people. Are there ways to eliminate or minimize your exposure to noise on the job? Earplugs or protective earphones may provide an answer for some people. Or you may be able to move to a soundproofed office.

If your occupation involves strenuous physical activity or if you work in a hot environment, you'll need to be careful to avoid becoming dehydrated. Have plenty of fluids on hand so that you can continually replace the body fluids you lose.

Are you one of those fortunate persons who works in an air-conditioned building? It can be a mixed blessing. The changes in air temperature when you leave or enter an air-conditioned area on a hot day may send you spinning. If it's possible to control the cooling system in your work place, keep the thermostat set in a moderate range instead of on "frigid."

Remember, too, that people with some types of balance disorders are often affected by changes in barometric pressure. So when the weather is changing rapidly, be alert to fluctuations in your condition.

You may be able to find ways to change your work environment so that you can be more productive and keep your symptoms to a minimum. The change may be as simple as the one John Wilson discovered.

John, a high school math teacher, had been recuperating at home for six weeks following his inner ear surgery. He was feeling well and, with his doctor's permission, returned to work. "I felt great in the morning, but by the middle of the day I was dizzy and nauseated," John said. "I tried to figure out what it was that made me feel dizzy so often. Finally a friend suggested that I move my desk to the other side of the room. I had been constantly turning my head toward my affected side when I got up to do some math problems on the blackboard. Once I moved the desk, I found that my symptoms disappeared."

Place your frequently used supplies at eye level where they are easy to reach. If you work in an area where there is lots of noise, movement, or confusion, keep your door closed, isolate yourself with a partition, or move your desk into a corner facing a wall. Be sure the people you work with understand the reason for the change so they don't think you're trying to avoid them.

If you have a hearing loss, you may need to use some hearing-assistive devices. Installing a flashing light on your office phone may prevent you from missing an important call. A telephone amplifier may be helpful, too. You can get more information on hearing-assistive devices from your audiologist. Helpful assistance is usually available from civic organizations such as Lions Clubs or Sertoma Clubs that have special affiliations with clinical and research hearing programs.

Work-related stress may be responsible for increasing your

symptoms. Try analyzing the stressful aspects of your job. What can you do to minimize them? Would a sympathetic co-worker or supervisor be able to help you make some changes? Organization, both at home and at work, will allow you to use your energy to the best advantage. Get organized now. You won't be sorry you took the time to do it.

Chapter 12

Living It Up

If you have been affected by dizziness for a while, you may have found it necessary to give up some of your favorite recreational activities. Maybe you've always spent every extra moment outdoors, tramping over mountain trails or strolling along ocean beaches. Now, mountain altitudes bring on nausea, sandy beaches provide unsteady footing, and the rolling surf causes waves of seasickness.

Perhaps you have had to resign from the company bowling team or give up your weekly tennis matches because you're so dizzy you can't focus on the ball. Maybe you can't even stand to work in your flower garden because every time you bend over, you lose your balance.

Once you uncover the reason for your dizziness and other symptoms, you can begin to discover ways to cope with them or even get rid of them. As you learn more about how you can adapt some of your favorite activities, your life will begin to return to normal. You'll be able to get out and live it up again.

Walking, Hiking

Walking is great exercise. It's a way to commune with nature. It's a pleasant social activity. When dizziness and imbalance bother you, there are a few precautions you should take.

Start out easy. Walk around the block, then around town. Begin on the sidewalks and graduate to hard dirt or jogging paths. Uneven surfaces may be difficult to handle at first, but as your symptoms diminish and your endurance increases, your confidence will return.

Be especially careful on slippery gravel, rough brick or cobblestone paths, and icy surfaces. You can compensate in part for an inability to depend on your sense of

Figure 12-1: Hiking is great exercise. You may want to use a hiking stick and have a person or dog with you to help you hear.

touch in these situations by using your eyes. Watch the ground more closely than usual and pay attention to where your feet will land.

Make walking a social occasion. Take along a friend on your first walk in the park or woods. Explain your difficulty with uneven surfaces so that he or she can be prepared to assist you.

A cell phone in your pocket might give you a little more confidence and another safety net of sorts.

Many people who are avid walkers carry beautiful handcrafted walking sticks.

Riding in Cars

Circular freeway ramps, circular parking garages, objects rushing by in your peripheral vision—these can present special problems to people affected by motion sickness and dizziness. If these situations provoke symptoms for you, the ideal solution is to avoid them. Certainly you shouldn't drive if your symptoms make driving dangerous. While it may not be possible to avoid all car travel, you may be able to manage your symptoms and ride comfortably in the passenger seat. People prone to motion sickness generally prefer the front seat.

Anti-motion sickness medications that help minimize your symptoms are available in drug stores and pharmacies. If you are taking any prescribed medications, be sure to check with your physician before using these or any other over-the-counter drugs.

Try this when you are a passenger in a car. Focus straight ahead or look at something inside the car. Avoid watching the scenery stream by through the side windows. Even when the car isn't moving, you will probably want to avoid watching traffic or a train passing by.

It probably will be difficult for you to read while you are in a moving car. Increased visual input from the words bouncing up and down before your eyes may be too much for your brain to handle. It might be best to let someone else read road maps, freeway signs, or street addresses.

Changes in altitude may affect some people with vestibular disorders. When traveling over mountain passes or down to sea level at the beach, be prepared for increased symptoms that may occur as the air pressure changes.

On long trips, be sure to take water and other emergency supplies. If you have an acute attack of dizziness, you can ask the driver to stop until your symptoms subside. Having a thermos of fluids, some cheese crackers or other snack foods, and a blanket and pillow can make the wait more comfortable.

Shopping

Crowds, noise, and a swirl of activity on every side can be troubling to a person affected by dizziness. Once you are feeling up to tackling the weekly grocery shopping, though, the charge to your favorite shopping mall won't be far behind. When starting out, try to do your shopping during the off hours in the stores. If you wait until five o-clock on Friday evening to finish off your grocery list, the bustle of the busy supermarket will be sure to wear you out—and fast. At quieter times of the day, you will be able to move more slowly through the aisles so that brightly-colored boxes and packages won't stream by in a dizzying array.

Avoid the usual "up one aisle, down the next" traffic pattern that most shoppers follow in the store. Instead, try varying your route to stay in the wider end aisles for awhile to give your senses a short break. You may find that this helps to eliminate some of the confusion of moving quickly through one crowded, narrow aisle after another.

Try visiting large shopping malls at quieter times, too. The noisy crowds, bright lights, and flowing lanes of pedestrian traffic may provoke episodes of dizziness at first. If you begin to feel unsteady, find a seat and take a rest. Focus on an object close to you. Have a quiet conversation with the friend you've brought along. Try to ignore the activity around you for awhile. Then get up and move on—preferably to a small quiet shop. Don't give up. Just remember to try to shop when the crowds are smallest and when you are rested. You'll be less apt to be disturbed by all the hustle and bustle. As you progress, you may find shopping less bothersome.

Exercise

Getting in shape is one of the best things you can do for yourself. Not only will you be healthier, you will be busy training your balance system at the same time.

If there are special exercise classes for people with balance disorders available in your area,

Figure 12-2: Exercise machines can help retrain your balance system.

you may want to start off with those. The exercises you'll be doing are designed to incorporate head movements that train your balance system to adapt to specific vestibular input. Consistent participation in these exercises helps many people recover their balance abilities faster.

Using a rowing machine involves repeated movements of the head and body and will speed up the retraining of your balance system.

Work up slowly to regular aerobics classes that involve toe touches and swinging your arms and head back and forth.

Be cautious when using a treadmill. Your sense of touch is minimized on the moving surface and it may be more difficult for you to maintain your balance.

Consider trying t'ai chi, a regimen of exercises practiced widely in China. It consists of slow rhythmic movement from one specific total body position to another done simultaneously with regulated breathing (breathing out slowly, etc.) If you have impaired balance, it will usually be more pronounced if you try to stay still or move slowly. T'ai chi forces you to hold a position or move very slowly, and this may give you the work on movement where you need it most.

Figure 12-3: Exercise classes enhance both physical and social fitness.

Favorite Sports

Participating in sports activities is an excellent way to keep in shape. It not only provides you with terrific exercise, but it's a great way to maintain contact with your friends. As long as you start slowly and work up to more strenuous friendly-competitive matches, there are many sports you'll be able to enjoy.

Figure 12-4: A softball team, whether a group of friends or fellow employees, offers both exercise and social contact.

Tennis, racquetball, basketball, squash, badminton, and handball involve repetitive head movements that really give your vestibular system a workout. Basketball might be the best one to try first because the ball is larger and easier to see. You may notice that turning toward the right or left, or looking up quickly causes more symptoms than other movements. As your playing time increases, however, this should diminish.

Volleyball may prove to be especially difficult for you to play if your symptoms occur when you throw your head back to look upward. Again, work up to it slowly.

Although bowling is not as strenuous as the sports mentioned above, it also involves repetitive head movements that help retrain your balance system.

You will need to be cautious when roller-skating or ice-skating. The information that your brain receives from the muscles and joints of your feet and legs isn't as reliable as it is when your feet are on solid ground. Even if you are an expert skater, it may be more difficult for you to maintain your balance.

Skiing may be out because riding a chairlift may be quite disorienting. Your vision in the snow isn't as sharp as it ought to be and it's difficult to depend on your sense of touch when your feet are inside heavy ski boots. Add to these handicaps a high mountain altitude and a swirling snowstorm, and you might find yourself in a real predicament.

If you find that you just can't manage downhill skiing, give cross-country skiing a try. The speed is slower. You'll avoid the dizzying heights on the chairlift. Your chance of injury is greatly reduced.

Water Sports

Swimming is terrific exercise too. Unless you have been diagnosed with BPPV or any vestibular disorder causing attacks of disabling vertigo and/or your doctor recommends against swimming, you should be able to participate as long as you follow two safety precautions. You should never swim alone, and you should avoid swimming at night

Figure 12-5: Swimming also offers both fitness and social contacts.

when you can't depend on vision to help you determine the direction to the surface of the pool or lake.

Motion at sea or on any kind of boat can cause seasickness in people with normal vestibular systems. If you are prone to episodes

Figure 12-6: Fishing from a float tube or raft, where you are closer to the surface of the water, may be easier than fishing from a boat. When you are low in the water, the horizon remains relatively steady.

of dizziness, your symptoms may be highly aggravated by the confusing input your brain receives when you are on a floating dock or a boat. Not all people with vestibular disorders are bothered by boat motion. If you are keen to try it, go on a short ride first, close to shore, before committing to a longer voyage.

Spectator Sports

There is no need to give up hope of attending stadium games. For basketball, try to buy seats near the ends of the courts and up high enough so that you can have the whole court in view at once. That way you can avoid frequent back-and-forth head movements that might tend to make you dizzy. Just remember that the noise level can reach tremendous heights as your favorite player soars in for a slam-dunk. If you are particularly sensitive to noise, a wide-screen TV may be the way to go. You might also check with your audiologist about using earplugs to lessen the impact of the noise.

No need to skip the tennis matches either. Here the noise is better controlled (usually), and if your seat is behind and above one of the players, you'll probably be just fine.

If your best friend invites you to the annual air show, or to an evening of stargazing, bring along your reclining lawn chair. You can relax and enjoy the show without having to throw your head back and jeopardize your balance.

Entertainment

When the show's about to begin and the lights go down, that's when you might be in trouble. Be sure you get there on time. The lighting is usually dim in theaters, and you'll need to be seated before the lights go out.

Sometimes movie soundtracks or concert music is much too loud to be tolerated by people who have inner ear disorders. If the noise or music is disturbing, you might find it helpful to use earplugs when you go to the theater or concert hall. Get in the habit of carrying them with you. You can use them to screen out excess noise in many situations.

Attending a concert? The symphony or a singer might be just great, but watch out for the rock show complete with dancing strobe lights. They are disabling to someone with a balance problem.

You might find that the same thing is true of video games. The bright lights, zooming blips, and whining screams of starships streaking across the screen could overwhelm your balance system with input.

So you opt for something intellectual. The community travelogue series seems harmless—until the speaker gets up, waves his lighted pointer through the air, switches his slides on and off, gestures wildly with his hands, and continually paces back and forth across the front of the room. Beware.

Travel

Many community transportation systems have special facilities for people who are unable to use public buses or trains. Transportation may be provided door-to-door for medical appointments, work, school, or as scheduling is available, to shopping and recreational activities. With documentation from your physician, you may qualify for a program that is available in your area.

Even though you are able to use public transportation, is traveling sometimes an ordeal? If so, here are some things you can do to make your next trip more pleasant.

When you travel by bus or train, be sure to get a seat that faces forward in the center of the vehicle. If there are no-smoking cars or areas, take advantage of them. Try to avoid commuter rush hours, when you might have to stand in a moving vehicle.

Thinking of flying to Tahiti? When you make your reservations, ask for a seat over the wing or near the center of the plane, where it is most stable. You won't be subjected to quite as much up-and-down motion.

The recirculated air in airplanes is very dry. Drink plenty of water and/or non-alcoholic decaffeinated beverages before and during your flight especially if it is more than two hours long.

Taking decongestants before you fly may help you avoid collapsed eustachian tubes that sometimes occur when the cabin pressure changes. Some people use devices like Ear Planes to lessen the sound and to slow down the pressure changes. Ask your physician for advice on managing this problem.

Plan ahead and allow yourself plenty of time on your day of departure. Airports can be crowded, confusing, and chaotic at times.

If you are unable to travel alone, Greyhound Lines, Inc., will make a special allowance for you and your companion. Under certain circumstances, you may be able to buy two tickets for the price of one. Call your local Greyhound office or visit the Greyhound web site at www.greyhound.com for more information.

You Can Do It!

Exercise and recreation are important parts of your life. As you get into shape and increase your activity, you'll find that you're feeling better all the time. The stress of coping with your dizziness symptoms will begin to decrease.

Some days it will take a tremendous effort just to get started. But keep going, gradually increasing your activity as though you are getting into condition for a sporting event. Do as much as you can. You'll find the effort will be well worthwhile as you begin to live it up again.

Spread the Word

If you told a friend that you had just been diagnosed with heart disease or cancer, he or she would have some understanding of your symptoms, your treatment, and your limitations. That friend might have read a recent article about it in *Time* or a daily newspaper. He or she has probably known someone else with a similar diagnosis and can sympathize with you.

People with inner ear disorders don't benefit from the same name familiarity. Your friend has probably never heard of BPPV or endolymphatic hydrops. Maybe your friend's grandmother's sister had Meniere's disease, but your friend has heard that Meniere's disease has something do with old age. Anyway, your friend probably thinks that, whatever you have, it can't be too bad because you don't look sick—your problem is probably "psychological."

Educate others about your disorder. If your family and friends know what your symptoms and limitations are, and if they are aware of situations that aggravate your condition, they can help you cope with the problems you face. They can begin to understand how you feel.

After Betty Finn was diagnosed with BPPV, she took the time to explain her condition to her friend. "Several times when you told me you were feeling dizzy, I thought you were using it as an excuse to stay home," Connie responded. "But now that I think about it, you often had a kind of glazed look in your eyes. You must have been trying to control that abnormal nystagmus."

Many people may not realize that a person with an inner ear disorder often has a related hearing problem (or vice versa). If you have trouble distinguishing speech, ask your friends to face you as they talk and to speak clearly. Be sure they recognize that you have more difficulty understanding them when there is a lot of background noise.

Some people may interpret forgetfulness or lack of concentration as a sign of inattention or rudeness on your part. It will help to explain that you sometimes feel confused when you are experiencing even a mild attack of dizziness.

Sometimes you may become very frustrated because people don't understand your physical problem, because you can't do everything you would like to do, or because your future seems so uncertain. At times like these, it helps to be able to express your frustration, to get it off your chest.

Try to find someone who has had similar experiences, who can lend an empathetic ear, and who can share ways that he has found to cope with the same problems that face you. Many such people belong to the Vestibular Disorders Association, an information and support organization founded in 1983 in Portland, Oregon This nonprofit organization sends information to every continent and includes members from around the globe. Although the group was originally composed primarily of patients at a single hospital in Portland, this nonprofit association now includes members worldwide.

The primary goal of the Vestibular Disorders Association is to provide information and a support network for people with dizziness and balance disorders. The bond that VEDA members have in common is an understanding of how it feels to have a physical disability that alters their lives and daily activities. They are able to share with others the problems and frustrations that they experience and the ways they have found to cope with them.

Education of members, their families, and the public is another goal of VEDA. The quarterly newsletter, *On the Level*, and a wide variety of brochures and fact sheets also help members learn about recent advances in diagnosis and treatment.

Here are VEDA's addresses and phone numbers:

Vestibular Disorders Association (VEDA)
P.O. Box 13305; Portland, OR 97213-0305
Phone: (800) 837-8428
Fax: (503) 229-8064
info@vestibular.org
www.vestibular.org

You are learning to cope with your dizziness problem. You sometimes feel terrible, but you don't look sick. You need to exercise, but you can't get over-tired. You can't eat too much salt, but you need to drink plenty of fluids. There are some things you just can't do, but your friends don't always understand.

It's a real balancing act. But you'll get better at it all the time!

Chapter 13

Where to Get More Information

Your first source of information about dizziness and balance disorders and their diagnosis, treatment, and effects should always be your doctor and members of his or her staff. Additional information can also be found through libraries and from patient support organizations, the Internet (whether or not you own a computer), and other people with similar problems.

Libraries

The library has always been a good place to go for information. This is true even in the age of the Internet. You can find information about vestibular disorders at the local hospital library, college library, and the closest medical school library. Your local library most likely won't have much about vestibular problems on its shelves but might be of help anyway.

Start with the librarian at your local library. She or he can make suggestions to help get you started. If the local library does not have the information you are looking for, the reference librarian or another librarian may be able to get it. Most libraries borrow books they don't own from libraries that have them (interlibrary loan). They can also help with access to the Internet.

Hospitals sometimes maintain medical libraries for their doctors and staffs, and sometimes these libraries are available for public use. On occasion, a hospital will have a library or a library section devoted to public education. These hospital libraries usually have a modest selection of books and scientific journals. Be prepared to do your own looking since hospital librarians may not have much time to assist you; their primary mission is to serve the hospital staff.

The local junior college may also have useful books and journals, particularly if it has a health care program for registered nurses, respiratory therapists, physical therapy assistants, or other health care professionals. Many four-year colleges and universities also have books, magazines, and scientific journals related to health care.

Medical schools usually have well-stocked medical libraries, and borrowing privileges may be available to the public. The information at these libraries will most likely be meant for graduate physicians, medical students, and students of other professional schools (nursing, audiology, physical therapy, pharmacy, occupational therapy, and dentistry) associated with the college. If you are interested in reading medical and other health care journals, go prepared to make copies; journals usually can't be checked out of the library but must be used on the premises. Although medical school librarians may not have time to help you as much as public librarians, most of the medical libraries include displays and brochures explaining where things are and how to find them.

Some private clinics also make vestibular materials available to the public. For example, if you live near Los Angeles, you might find what you are looking for in the otology library at the House Ear Institute.

Organizations

A few organizations offer information to people about dizziness and balance disorders.

The Vestibular Disorders Association (VEDA) has a large collection of non-technical printed information, including full-length books about Meniere's disease and BPPV, as well as DVDs. Its web site (www.vestibular.org) provides a substantial amount of objective educational information about symptoms, the balance system, diagnosis, and treatment; contact information for local support groups; a searchable provider directory of health specialists who diagnose and treat vestibular disorders; and links to related organizations, government sites, professional certifying boards, online discussion groups, and other helpful resources. In addition, VEDA's web site includes an online store (https://vestibular.org/shop/) that offers visitors the ability to review summaries of all educational publications available and make any desired purchases for delivery.

Patient Support Organizations

Brain Injury Association
(800) 444-6443
www.biausa.org

National Stroke Association
9907 E. Easter Lane; Englewood, CO 80112
(800) 787-6537
www.stroke.org

Vestibular Disorders Association (VEDA)
P.O. Box 13305; Portland, OR 97213-0305
(800) 837-8428 (24-hour answering machine)
www.vestibular.org

Professional Organizations

American Academy of Neurology (AAN)
1080 Montreal Ave.; St. Paul, MN 55116
(800) 879-1960
www.aan.com

American Academy of Otolaryngology-Head and Neck Surgery
One Prince Street; Alexandria, VA 22314-3357
(703) 836-4444
www.entnet.org

American Physical Therapy Association
1111 N. Fairfax Street; Alexandria, VA 22314-1488
(800) 999-2782; TTY: (703) 683-6748
www.apta.org

American-Speech-Language-Hearing Association (ASHA)
2200 Research Blvd.; Rockville, MD 20850
Toll-free, voice or TTY: (800) 638-8255
www.asha.org

U. S. Government

National Library of Medicine
8600 Rockville Pike; Bethesda, MD 20894
(888) 346-3656
www.nlm.nih.gov

NIDCD Information Clearinghouse
1 Communication Ave.; Bethesda, MD 20892-3456
(800) 241-1044; TDD/TT: (800) 241-1055
www.nidcd.nih.gov/

NIDCD National Temporal Bone, Hearing, and Balance Pathology Resource Registry
Massachusetts Eye and Ear Infirmary
243 Charles St.; Boston, MA 02114-3096
(800) 822-1327; TTY: (888) 561-3277
www.tbregistry.org

Social Security Administration
(Check the telephone Yellow Pages for information on your local Social Security Administration branch office.)
(800) 772-1213; TTY: (800) 325-0778
www.ssa.gov

Internet

If you have a computer and Internet access, you are probably already familiar with news groups, electronic mailing lists, web pages, and other electronic communication modes. Most of these modes can provide access to information about dizziness and balance disorders. If you don't have a computer, try your local library. Most libraries have Internet access, and librarians can help you find things on the Internet.

If you don't have a computer, you can also ask neighbors and relatives who may have Internet access or know someone who does. Most people using the Internet would probably be happy to help you find information; part of their fun is the hunt.

Also, your town may have a "cyber cafe," a retail business offering Internet access in a coffeehouse setting.

Kinds of information

The Internet includes an enormous amount of information. The U.S. Federal government has huge sites, including those of the Social Security Administration, the National Institute on Deafness and Other Communication Disorders (NIDCD), the National Institutes of Health (NIH), the National Library of Medicine (NLM), the Library of Congress and more. Information from many organizations, colleges and universities, hospitals, doctors, and individuals are available on the Internet. Many publishers of professional medical journals list the tables of contents of their journal issues; some even include summaries of the articles.

Government forms and publications are available "on-line" including booklets from the Social Security Administration. You can download them and print them immediately without writing a letter and waiting for a reply.

Books in print are listed at the Library of Congress Internet site, and medical books in print are listed at the NLM site.

A handful of universities have posted on-line textbooks containing basic anatomy and physiology of the ear and other ear information, including graphics, at their web sites.

If you want to read current scientific papers on vestibular disorders, you can look for abstracts and bibliographic information on the Internet using MEDLINE, a database of the NLM. You can use the PubMed version on-line for free. MEDLINE contains more than 8.8 million references to articles published in 3,800 biomedical journals. Many of these references include 300-word abstracts as well as the names of titles, authors, publishers, and other bibliographic information. You can search MEDLINE at home or at work using your own computer and Internet connection, or you can use on-line services at libraries or other institutions offering web access to the public. To connect to PubMed or to find out more about it and other NLM services, go to the web page at www.nlm.nih.gov. Health care professionals and researchers as well as the general public use MEDLINE and related databases.

Electronic Mailing Lists

To join an electronic mailing list that includes people with vestibular disorders, you must subscribe (for free) via e-mail. You must follow subscription directions exactly since a computer, not a person, handles the entire process. Unless you write the appropriate command in the correct place with the correct spelling, your e-mail subscription request will fail. If you are unsuccessful the first time, check your word placement and spelling. Delete all extraneous material, such as your automated signature lines, from your message. Here is an example:

Dizzinews Mailing List
To: majordomo@samurai.com
From: your e-mail address
Subject: (leave blank)
Message: subscribe dizzinews

Fill in the blanks as instructed and send the e-mail. The mailing list computer will send back a message to announce that you are subscribed and to tell you how the group works and how to quit the list (unsubscribe). Keep these instructions; save them on disk, and print a copy. You will need these instructions later if you want to unsubscribe.

Don't write anything to a group that you would not want on the front page of your local newspaper. Most e-mails sent to an entire group or mailing list are saved for anyone to read at any time.

VEDA compiles and maintains lists of these Internet mailing lists, chat rooms, and on-line support groups. For more information, visit www.vestibular.org/links.php.

Link Lists

Not everyone has a computer or access to the Internet. For those who prefer a pen-pal list printed on paper, VEDA maintains a Link List for members located all around the world. People who join VEDA may participate in this optional service by adding their names and contact information (e.g., mailing address, telephone number, and/or e-mail address) to the Link List. They will then receive a printout of the entire worldwide list of participants.

Glossary

Acoustic neuroma. Tumor of the vestibulo-cochlear nerve. Also called acoustic neurinoma or schwannoma.

Arteriosclerosis. Hardening of the arteries.

Balance. State of repose between two or more antagonistic forces that exactly counteract each other. Equilibrium.

Benign paroxysmal positional vertigo (BPPV). Syndrome or disorder involving episodes of vertigo occurring with particular head movements. Sometimes also called BPV (benign positional vertigo) or BPPN (benign paroxysmal positional nystagmus).

Bilateral. Involving both ears.

Brainstem. Part of the brain that performs motor, sensory, and reflex functions.

Caloric test. A test that requires irrigation of the ear canal with warm and/or cool water or air to measure vestibular functions.

Cerebellum. Part of the brain responsible for muscle coordination.

Cerebral cortex. Part of the brain that controls voluntary movements and coordinates thinking and memory.

Cholesteatoma. Cyst-like growth that occurs most commonly in the middle ear.

Cochlea. End organ of hearing.

Cupula. Gelatinous mass covering the hair cells in the ampulla of a semicircular canal.

Disequilibrium. Vague sense of unsteadiness, imbalance, tilting, or bumping into things that can occur in association with vestibular disorders.

Dix-Hallpike test. Maneuver to see if nystagmus occurs during certain changes in head position. The test is useful in diagnosing BPPV.

Ear drum. Common name for the tympanic membrane. It forms the boundary between the outer and middle ears.

Effusion. Escape of fluid from the blood vessels or lymphatics into tissues or a cavity.

Electronystagmography (ENG). A method of measuring eye movements. A battery of ENG tests, including the caloric ENG, may be used to assess relationships between the eyes and the vestibular system and help diagnose the cause of dizziness or vertigo.

Endolymph. Fluid contained within the semicircular canals, the vestibule, and the cochlea of the inner ear.

Endolymphatic hydrops. Excessive amount of endolymph. Increased pressure from this endolymph can damage any part of the vestibular apparatus or the cochlea.

Eustachian tube. Hourglass-shaped tube connecting the middle ear with the area of the throat behind the nose. The tube is usually closed but opens during swallowing or yawning, allowing an exchange of air. This equalizes the pressure between the middle ear and the outside.

Hair cells. Sensory receptors of the vestibular system; located in the macular organs and the cupula of each semicircular canal.

Hyperventilation. Over-breathing. Condition in which breathing becomes deep and rapid and too much carbon dioxide is exhaled.

Idiopathic. Of unknown cause.

Inner ear. Fluid-filled system of chambers and passageways encased in the temporal bone. The inner ear includes the end organs of hearing and balance and is also called the labyrinth.

Labyrinth. Complex series of chambers and passageways of the inner ear, including the hearing and balance parts.

Labyrinthitis. Inflammation of the labyrinth or part of it.

Macula. Patch of hair cells in either the saccule or utricle; covered with a gelatinous material containing otoliths.

Mal de debarquement. Rare vertigo condition in which people develop a prolonged landsickness, often lasting months, after an ocean cruise or other form of prolonged motion.

Meniere's disease. Vestibular disorder of unknown cause which occurs at intervals and is characterized by vertigo, tinnitus, a feeling of fullness in the ear, and fluctuating hearing loss.

Middle ear. Part of the ear that reaches from the eardrum to the outer surfaces of the oval and round windows.

Migraine. Symptom complex occurring periodically and character-ized by pain in the head, vertigo, nausea, vomiting, photophobia, and scintillating appearances of light.

Motion sickness. Feeling of nausea and/or dizziness triggered by movement, usually in a car, boat, airplane, or carnival ride.

Neurologist. Medical doctor who has undergone four years of resi-dency training in medical problems of the brain, nervous system, and nerves.

Neuro-otologist. Otolaryngologist concerned mainly with the inner ear.

Neuropathy. Disorder affecting any segment of the nervous system.

Nystagmus. Involuntary, coordinated eye movement that occurs as your head moves or as your eyes follow a moving object.

Orthostatic hypotension. Form of low blood pressure that typically occurs during rapid movement from a sitting or lying posture to a standing posture.

Oscillopsia. Visual illusion that stationary objects are bobbing to and fro, back and forth, or up and down.

Osteoarthritis. Degenerative joint disease.

Otic capsule. Outer shell of the bony labyrinth.

Otolaryngologist. Medical doctor who specializes in disorders of the head and neck, especially those related to the ear, nose, and throat. This doctor may also be referred to as an otolaryngologist—head and neck surgeon, an ear-nose-throat (ENT) doctor, or an ENT specialist.

Otoliths. Calcium carbonate crystals stuck to the otolithic mem-brane of the utricle and saccule. Sometimes also called *ear rocks*.

Otologist. Otolaryngologist concerned with the entire ear.

Ototoxic. Poisonous to the ear. A substance that affects hearing or vestibular function.

Oval window. One of two covered openings between the middle ear and the inner ear. The footplate of the stapes rests in the oval window.

Perilymph fistula. Vestibular disorder caused by an abnormal opening between the middle-ear space and the fluid-filled inner ear.

Peripheral. Away from the center. In the context of vestibular disorders, refers to the inner ear as opposed to the brain or brainstem.

Proprioceptors. Specialized nerve endings located in muscles and around joints that are sensitive to touch, pressure, and movement of the muscle tissue surrounding them.

Round window. Membrane-covered opening between the middle ear and the inner ear.

Saccule. Part of the vestibular system containing sensory receptors that are sensitive to changes in head motion with respect to earth vertical.

Semicircular canal. Curved inner ear structure containing an organ that detects angular head movement. Each ear has three semicircular canals that lie perpendicular to one another, each in a different plane.

Sinusitis. Inflammation of any of the air cavities in the skull opening into the nasal cavities.

Spatial disorientation. Confusion about one's position in space. This might include confusion about the location of vertical and horizontal.

Stapes. Innermost of the three bones of the middle ear. It is sometimes referred to as the *stirrup* because of its shape.

Temporal bone. Part of the skull that houses the outer, middle, and inner ears.

Tinnitus. Hissing, ringing, or other abnormal noises in the ear. Commonly called "ringing in the ears."

Unilateral. Involving only one ear.

Utricle. Part of the vestibular system containing sensory receptors that are sensitive to changes in head motion with respect to earth horizontal.

Vasovagal syndrome. Nervous system response that causes sudden loss of muscle tone in peripheral blood vessels. A vasovagal attack results in pooling of blood in the legs and trunk and may reduce blood flow to the brain.

Vertigo. Perception of movement (either of yourself or of objects around you) that is not occurring or is occurring differently from what you perceive.

Vestibular. Related to the balance parts of the inner ear and related structures.

Vestibulo-cochlear nerve. Nerve from the brain that is essential to the senses of hearing and balance. Also called the *eighth cranial nerve, auditory nerve,* or *acoustic nerve.*

Vestibulo-ocular reflex (VOR). Involuntary eye movements caused by stimulating the vestibular system.

Vestibulo-spinal reflex (VSR). Involuntary movements caused by stimulating the vestibular system.

Index

Bold page numbers refer to definitions; italic page numbers refer to illustrations.

A

ABR *(see* auditory response test)
acoustic nerve, 33
acoustic neuroma, 33-34, 40, **83**
acoustic reflex threshold test, 26
active, staying, 50-52, 74-75
aging, 16, 29, 33
airplanes, 73
alcohol, 34, 58
allergies, 16, 52
allowable charge, 43
alprazolam, 36
American Academy of Neurology, 79
American Academy of
   Otolaryngology-Head and Neck
   Surgery, 79
American Heart Association, 56, 60
American Physical Therapy
   Association, 79
American Speech-Language-Hearing
   Association, 79
aminoglycoside antibiotics, 34
anti-anxiety drugs, 36
antibiotics, 30
antihistamines, 30
anti-motion sickness medications, 68
anti-nausea medications, 36
Antivert, 17, 36
anti-vertiginous medications, 30
anti-viral medications, 30, 36
arteriosclerosis, 19, **83**
aspirin, 34
Ativan, 36
attack, 22, 47, 52, 62, 68
   BPPV, 29
   managing, 47, 68
   Meniere's, 31
   migraine, 32
audiologists, 26, 64, 72
auditory brainstem response test, 28
auditory nerve, *10*
aura *(see* warning)

authorization, 42
auto-rotational testing, *27*

B

bacterial infection, 15
BAER *(see* auditory response test)
balance, 9, 15, 18, 28, 61, **83**
   and the brain, 9, 12
   compensate for imbalance, 38
   examination, 25, 26
   inner ear and, 10, 29, 32
   and movement exam, 25
   normal, 9, 13
   strategies, 38
   testing, 25-26, 28
   and vision, 9, 13, 61
balance center, 9, 12, 13
balance disorders, 8, 37, 39, 41, 48,
   58, 69, 74
balance systems, 9-13, 28, 69
   (see also proprioception; vestibular;
   vision)
barometric pressure changes, 64
Bell's palsy, 34
Benadryl, 36
benign paroxysmal positional vertigo
   (see BPPV)
benzodiazepines, 36
benzothiazide *(see* thiazide diuretics)
BER *(see* auditory response test)
bilateral, 15, 31, 83
blood flow to the inner ear, 31-32
blood pressure, low *(see* orthostatic
   hypotension)
blood sugar levels, 58
bone conduction test, 26
Bonine, 17, 36
bony labyrinth, 10
bouncing vision *(see* oscillopsia)
BPPV, 15, 16, **29**, 71, 78, **83**
brain, 7, 9, 12, 13, 18, 19, 25, 51
   examination, 25, 28
   and nervous system exam, 25

S

T